Without this book, you and I would be missing a great chapter in the saga of modern service to the Lord. We are indebted to Donna Thomas for retelling the story of this man of God and his trailblazing work around the world. These stories give a fresh vision for helping people reach out for what the Lord has for them and become personally engaged in reaching their world for him.

Dr. John D. Fozard, President
Mid-America Christian University

In life, I have found that you never know who is watching you, who looks to you as a model and mentor. I'm sure that Chuck Thomas never knew that I, as a Wichita teenager, was watching with amazement and wonder. He clearly was a man far ahead of his time. Audacious, visionary, and almost appearing to be impulsive, he made a huge impact on many young people like me. His life and legacy are proof that you get great things done for the kingdom by taking chances, living and thinking outside the box, and thereby changing the world in the process. I'm so glad that Donna has chronicled this life of faith and adventure so that Chuck Thomas will continue to inspire and challenge those whose lives are touched by his story.

Dr. Jay A. Barber, Jr., President Emeritus
Warner Pacific College

Those who wonder if ministry is an adventure need to know about Chuck Thomas. He was a man of remarkable talent, vision, courage, and creativity whose selfless dedication made a profound difference for the cause of Christ in his fascinating years of ministry that spanned the globe. His ministry reached untold millions. He took many on his journeys of service, and they also would never be the same. Donna Thomas, Chuck's life partner, gives to us a true story worth reading and casts light on a life worth emulating. This is an encouraging witness to God's faithfulness through a life richly lived that has made an enormous difference for the sake of the kingdom.

Dr. James L. Edwards, President
Anderson University

Throughout the decades, God at times calls individuals to be innovative and think outside the box. In Charles Thomas I see an individual called and committed to the Lord first and foremost. Reading his adventures with the Lord can inspire us as we glean the positive attributes of his life lived for Christ.

Ron Duncan, General Director
Church of God Ministries

Chuck Thomas was a man of great vision. His life story is compelling. Long before eyewitness mission tours became an integral part of congregational mission, Chuck Thomas was leading the way. A faithful churchman, loyal soldier, committed minister, and loving husband and father, Chuck allowed his passion for others to fuel everything he did. Many people around the world are indebted to Chuck because of his untiring efforts to get people outside the walls of the church to discover what God is doing in the world. It was my privilege to know and follow the ministry of Chuck and Donna. They have truly been the Aquila and Priscilla of our generation

David Sebastian, Dean, School of Theology
Anderson University

Here is a book that can be enjoyed on so many levels by so many readers. It's an adventure story, unfolding in far corners of the world; a biography, tracing the life and works of a visionary leader; and a romance, illustrating a couple's commitment to each other and to the global ministry they built. Best of all, this is a guidebook that teaches what a missional lifestyle looks like and how each of us has the capacity to live it.

Holly Miller, author, editor, professional-in-residence
Anderson University

Chuck Thomas was a giant … his influence for Christ looms … from Indiana to India … North, South, East, and West … from people movements to moving people … and now we can once again benefit from his life. His faithful wife and partner-with-equal-zest, Donna Thomas, brings before us a vivid portrait of a person who believed he belonged to God and lived that way. As you read, may you be challenged and encouraged to do the same!

Dr. Steve Rennick, Senior Pastor
Church at the Crossing, Indianapolis, IN

Though I never met Chuck Thomas in person, I feel after reading his story that I know him and am awed by the influence he had on so many people. Chuck's story should be a tremendous inspiration and a challenge to everyone who reads it to look for another door when one closes. Chuck's life was an amazing testament to a person's ability to listen to God and do amazing works. When we look at all the mission trips taking place around the world today, knowing that they started with a small seed that Chuck planted, I cannot help but be inspired and challenged to listen more closely to God and ask what he would have me do to spread His Word. Donna, thank you for sharing Chuck with the world.

Robert W. Lazard, CPA
Indianapolis, IN

Conversations with Chuck always included the "why not factor." Chuck had a way of shining a spotlight on opportunity. Frequently he would turn the conversation toward a subtle question: "What significant event has happened in your ministry?" He would listen intently and follow up with: "That's terrific … now toss your leaders a bigger challenge!" Read Donna Thomas' unique narrative of the life of Charles Thomas not so much for the joy of memories but for the challenges you'll discover, as I did, between the lines.

D. Dewayne Repass, Chief Development Officer
Church of God Ministries

Chuck Thomas lived a life of total commitment to Christ and the Great Commission. With radical obedience he exemplified the missional church at its best. Your faith will be inspired as you read the real life account of one who took God's call personally and responded obediently by going into all the world.

Arlo F. Newell, Editor in Chief, Retired
Warner Press

THE "WHY NOT?" FACTOR

CHUCK THOMAS, TRAILBLAZER

DONNA S. THOMAS

Cover design and photo: Joe Pagliaro
Editor: Karen Roberts

 Mid-America Christian University Press
Oklahoma City, Oklahoma
www.MACU.edu

For permission to use material, contact:
Donna Thomas
Christian Vision Ministries
2460 Glebe Street, Suite 216
Carmel, IN 46032
Email: donnathomas29@att.net
Website: www.cvministries.org

Dedication

This book is gratefully dedicated to every person who chooses the "Why not?" factor in their walk with the Lord.

Contents

Foreword

The writing of a person's story is so important to the development of our culture. It is impossible for us to know on a personal level all of the great people by which we are surrounded. Therefore, the gift of their life stories, told through the eyes of someone who knew them well, is priceless. From them we can learn valuable lessons to help us in our own life journey.

Someone has said, "Nothing is meaningful without a context." We receive a rich context of a life lived when a family member writes the story. Donna Thomas, in this writing, is offering us the gift of her husband's life. She adds to it the rich context of their lives lived together as they fell in love, served in love, and grew in love.

You will be blessed by the tireless love they had for their work, the love for adventure that took them around the world, and the love for God that empowered them to enrich the lives of thousands.

It is important for us to read the stories of others' lives to learn how they faced hardships, handled their critics, solved their conflicts, lived their dreams, dealt with disappoint, and survived success. As you read the life stories of others, you discover how they organized their lives and lived out their stewardship. Reading the life story of Charles F. Thomas will provide you with insight into how two persons, committed to one another and to the Lord, can make a difference in the world. You will be challenged to dream bigger, try harder, and depend on God all the more.

We have but one life to live. It was my joy to have lived a portion of my life with Charles Thomas. He was a dear friend, a mentor, a brother in Christ, and a very real human being. I am grateful to his wife, Donna, for putting on the page a clearer picture of their lives together. This book will add context for all of us as we endeavor to live our lives to bring glory to God.

Rev. Claude Robold
Senior Pastor
New Covenant Church
Middletown, Ohio

Preface

I just hung up the phone. The call to come and speak, telling my life story, sent my mind racing back through memories. Do I have a story to tell that will bless and encourage others in their journey? Pondering the request, I realized the answer is yes, and it started with marrying an amazing man named Charles Thomas.

Chuck, that is what I call him, taught me to accept a challenge. Look outside the box. If one door is closed, find another one. He lived the "why not?" principle. I have quite a life story because of the influence and encouragement of Chuck Thomas. When I met him in 1946, he was just one of those G.I.'s returning from WWII. I soon realized how truly fortunate I was that he chose me to be his wife. Who would expect a new groom to build a house for his new bride while he was still in college? Who would expect a new graduate to plant a church? Who would be crazy enough to get a bus and then a 40- passenger airplane to start short-term missions ministry? Who, but I'm getting ahead of the story.

Why am I writing this story, the story of Chuck Thomas? There are lessons to be learned and new things yet ahead for every one of us. The Lord can use any of us willing to step up and say, "Here I am. Send me."

Countless people remember Chuck Thomas' entrepreneurial spirit. He would look at every problem as an opportunity. In searching for solutions, he would often find new and different ways of providing answers. He wouldn't question why something should be done, but why not. He was certainly ahead of his time in many of his answers.

Chuck's passion was for sharing the love of Christ and building the kingdom of God. His purpose was to be a committed disciple of Jesus Christ during his lifetime. To him that meant sharing the joy of salvation; caring for the hungry, needy, and sick; encouraging God's messengers; and enlisting others to join the corps of disciples committed to following the Lord wherever and whenever He led. Chuck used his sixty-eight years as a man of integrity, honor, and vision to follow the Lord and inspire others to do so. One theme of his life that he repeated often was, "God wants us to be, not to perform. Performance is a by-product of being." Chuck was certainly a grand example of a trailblazer. Challenged to do things that had never been done before and he set out to do them trusting others to follow in his footsteps and serve the Lord in their time.

The passion to serve God in whatever ways he could emerged from the dedication and character of his parents, his commitment to the Lord as a teenager, and especially his experiences with the Lord on the battlefield during World War II. He was one of few in his battalion who made it home alive, and he knew that the Lord had special plans for his life. Though he had previously considered being a physician, after the war he knew he was to be a pastor, one to bring people to know the Lord.

This writing is an attempt to chronicle the life of Chuck Thomas as a lasting memory of a man who used his time and talents for the Lord. It is a challenge to all who read it also to be trailblazers, following the special plan the Lord has just for you.

Acknowledgments

This book is the product of many people who have poured their hearts and their time into bringing it to reality. How thankful I am for their help. I especially want to acknowledge the valuable reading, editing, and encouragement of Karen Roberts. Simply stated, without her efforts, this book would not be here. Bob Lazard has been especially helpful in his editing and analyzing the different stories. Bob Leis' remembrances after World War II add a unique view of what life was like in those days. Jon and Lorna Kardatzke's thoughts and help are another blessing. And what a blessing to have Joe Pagliaro's valuable time and effort in this unique cover design.

There are numerous friends in different periods of time I also want to acknowledge, including those from the Pawnee Church pastoring days in Wichita; the Project Partner teams and groups, both in Wichita, Kansas, and in Middletown, Ohio; and the valuable endorsements of Enrique Cepeda, Ali Velasquez, Samuel Stephens, Lam Yam Man, Joe Surin, Guillermo Villanueva, Lener Cauper, Andrey Bondarenko, Eugen Groza, Peter Dugulescu, and Miguel Pinell.

A special thanks goes to Mid-America Christian University and President Dr. John Fozard for ordering this history and encouraging me to make it available for both young and old Christians seeking to do the will of the Lord and to choose the "Why not?" factor.

My deep appreciation goes to Chuck's and my special friend, Rev. Claude Robold, for his encouragement and for writing the Foreword and Afterword, valuable parts of the story. And especially I am thankful for my Board of Directors, Mary Mandel, Holly Miller, and Paula Quinn, enabling me to do this ministry with their endorsement and encouragement.

Other books by Donna S. Thomas

Through the Eyes of Christ: A Short-term Missions Journal

Climb Another Mountain

*Becoming a World Changing Family: Fun and Innovative Ways
to Spread the Good News*

*Faces in the Crowd: Reaching Your International Neighbor
for Christ*

Charles F. Thomas

Chapter One
AN UNBELIEVABLE ADVENTURE

"Who would be calling this early on Saturday?" Chuck said as he answered the phone.

"Are you aware that your airplane is down in Cuba?" said the voice on the other end of the phone.

"What are you talking about? Who is this?" Chuck inquired.

"This is the U.S. State Department, and we just received word that your plane has been forced down in Cuba."

"You've got to be kidding! We had clearance to overfly. Cuba gave us permission. Right now our plane is supposed to be on its way back to Fort Lauderdale and then Akron, Ohio. What do you mean it has been forced down in Cuba?"

"Sir, your plane was forced to land in Camaguay, Cuba, just twenty minutes ago. We don't know anything more but will be in touch with you. Stand by, and we'll call as soon as we have more information."

Chuck sent a look of shock my way, grabbed his coat, and yelled as he ran out the door, "I'll be at the office. Have them call me there. This is going to be a monumental problem. We have thirty-eight people on that plane besides our crew, and their lives are at stake. And call the prayer team. We've got to be ready for whatever."

This mission trip was one of the best Chuck and I had ever put together. It was 1974, and we had people from four different countries working together. People from Canada joined with a team in Canton, Ohio. They flew to Jamaica. There they left twelve of the team to work on a church and picked up twelve Jamaicans to go with them to work on a school in Haiti. Both of the projects were very successful and rewarding, especially so because Christians of four different nationalities had worked side by side.

As the president and founder of Project Partner with Christ, Chuck Thomas worked hard to ensure the safety of the teams we sent on short-term mission trips. He had obtained permission from the Cuban authorities to overfly Cuba on the Camaguay corridor as he had many times previously for our trips in the Caribbean. Cuba had our passenger manifest, the list of passengers, as was required.

On the day to come home, the crew first returned to Jamaica, dropped off the Jamaicans, and picked up the U.S. and Canadian team members they'd left there. They then headed north for Florida. But the return trip to the U.S. was not what anyone could ever have anticipated.

As the flight approached Cuba, the crew suddenly encountered three Russian MIGs. They were jet warplanes sent out by the Cuban government to intercept our plane. The MIGs began circling our plane, causing turbulence and havoc with their jet blasts. Dick Sanders and Don Shaver, the pilots on this trip, realized that one of the MIGs pulled right alongside Dick's window and started dropping and raising its landing gear, the international military signal to land.

Russian Mig

Great fear settled on everyone in the plane. Claude Ferguson, the team leader, got on the microphone. He led everybody on the plane in praying for God's intervention and protection in whatever lay ahead. The crew and team were totally at the mercy of the Cuban government. Then an amazing thing happened. Through the power of prayer, almost instantaneously, the pandemonium subsided. The Lord blessed them with his peace. Immediately calm settled over the entire plane. Some of the people even pulled out their cameras and took pictures of the MIGs since they were flying so close to our Convair 240, the 40-passenger airplane Chuck had purchased for short-term mission trips.

Although calm had returned, the crew and the passengers knew that they were still in great danger. Upon landing in Camaguay as they were instructed, the crew was taken to a room for interrogation. The team members were ushered into a large room where the exact number of chairs had been placed for the group. Since the Cuban officials had the flight manifest, they and even President Fidel Castro himself, we later learned, knew exactly how many people were on the plane.

That Saturday afternoon, State Department officials kept Chuck's office phone busy with conversations covering the demands Cuba was making in exchange for the release of the plane and passengers. The initial demand was for $3,000 in cash to be sent immediately via Western Union to the Swiss Embassy in Washington, D.C. Three hours later, another ransom request came for $5,000 and again in cash. Chuck didn't have that kind of money, and neither did Project Partner, but with the help of the Lord and the president of our local bank, Chuck was able to obtain the money immediately. Just getting it was a miracle in itself, since both police officers and electric company workers had to be brought in to open the bank vault.

The media got in the midst of the situation too. All three phone lines at the office rang throughout the night. First it was the local media. Then Chuck fielded calls from the *Miami Herald, New York Times, Los Angeles Times*, and numerous other newspapers in cities across the United States. Calls came from ABC, NBC, and CBS, all wanting an update on the story and what Chuck was going to do. This event was front-page news in Europe, South America, and across Asia. By Sunday morning, it seemed the whole world knew about the "Christian Plane Down in Cuba."

The State Department officials told Chuck to expect Castro to hold the team and crew for a minimum of two weeks, and it would probably be three or four. They wouldn't even estimate how much more money Castro would demand, but they did assure him that each time it would be a considerable amount and would always need to be sent immediately. They were, however, not counting on the Lord's intervention. Christians from everywhere had been calling too, telling us they were praying. By Sunday afternoon, just twenty-five hours after the incident began, the State Department called with miraculous news. Our plane had been released and was on its way to Fort Lauderdale, Florida.

It was a miracle. A tremendous miracle with effects that would last for years. Nobody was hurt. Project Partner received tons of publicity. Yes, it cost $8,000 in cold cash, but when people found out about the deficit, they sent their responses to meet the need. The gifts that came in totaled $4,000 beyond Castro's demand. So what did Chuck Thomas do in response to this incident? A few weeks later, he contacted a pastor in Canada, who had been to Cuba to encourage the Christians, and asked him if he was planning another trip. Yes. Would he take the $4,000 that had been given to Project Partner and give it to the Christian brothers in Cuba? Yes. An amazing way to help our Christian brothers and sisters in a closed communist country. Not part of our plan when we sent out that team, but obviously part of God's plan.

A great adventure. A great experience. A great miracle. It reassured Chuck again that he was on the right track. The things that had happened were all man's plans, but the Lord was in charge. He was ordering Chuck's steps.

Who Is This Chuck Thomas?

Charles F. Thomas was an ordinary man who pastored a church in Wichita, Kansas. He was a husband and father of three sons. But he was also the founder and president of a unique and innovative ministry. His concern for people in his community, throughout the United States, and in other countries stirred his heart and challenged him constantly to find new ways to serve them.

Chuck Thomas exemplified what Christian leaders today are calling a *missional lifestyle*. The term *missional* is new to the Christian world. To put it simply, *missional* calls us to find new ways of "being the church," being the people of God instead of "doing church." Charles Thomas lived a missional life, yet he never knew that term. He was the definition of win-win before Franklin Covey appeared on the scene and made the term famous. God blessed Chuck Thomas with a vision to serve him, and he in turn lived to bless millions around the world with God's love and compassion.

Countless people also remember the entrepreneurial spirit of this man. He would look at a problem as an opportunity. In searching for a solution, he would find new and different ways of providing an answer. He wouldn't question why his ideas should be done, but instead say, "why not?" Yes, his answer was always a challenging "why not?"

Chuck's passion was for sharing the love of Christ and building the kingdom of God. His life's purpose was to be a committed disciple of Jesus Christ. To him that purpose meant sharing the joy of salvation; caring for the hungry, the needy, and the sick; encouraging God's messengers; and enlisting others to join the core of workers committed to the Lord.

Chuck used his sixty-eight years as a man of integrity, honor, and vision to live his passion and fulfill his purpose. His theme was, "God wants us to love him and serve him, not to perform. What we accomplish is a by-product of loving God, loving others, and serving him above all else." He gave us a grand example, trusting others to follow in his footsteps and serve the Lord in their time.

Problems and adversity can beat people down. Difficult circumstances can cause us to lose our focus on God. Not so with Chuck Thomas. His passion emerged from his experiences with the Lord in the foxholes in France during World War II. It was there he saw that the Lord had a special plan for his life. And it was there he made a commitment to do the Lord's work every way possible. He saw his relationship with Jesus Christ as very precious, which caused him always to be thinking up new things to do and new ways to do them. Many of his plans were unheard of and on the verge of the impossible. He set new patterns, new ideas in front of ordinary people, giving them opportunities they never imagined. As a result, his life impacted hundreds of thousands, possibly millions of people for the Lord.

One of Chuck's unique gifts was in building teams. He did it as a pastor; he did it as the leader and visionary of Project Partner. He did it in our marriage and family. He raised three sons to follow his principles in their lives. And he brought me from a shy, young girl to be a team player with him around the world, yes, around the world. I would never have been able to accomplish what I have if Chuck Thomas hadn't been my guide, my mentor, and my encourager.

What's Ahead?

God always has adventures ahead for each of us. He certainly had many more adventures ahead for this Chuck Thomas: pastor, missionary innovator, faith builder, and adventurer. Chuck didn't know God's plans for his life as he was serving on the front line during WWII and learning to listen and lean on the Lord. He didn't realize what his parents had put in his heart with their decision to follow the Lord. He hadn't thought of planting a church and being a Christian innovator. He wasn't interested in missions. He didn't know he would be wild enough to get a 40-passenger airplane and take people where the Lord directed. He hadn't heard of short-term mission trips because they hadn't been thought of yet. He hadn't dreamed as to how to handle the military when they would meet him with their machine guns and fixed bayonets, or what to do with a stowaway on his plane. He didn't know he would be ready with a Christian Woodstock. He didn't think of adventures in China and impacting Chinese leaders. He didn't know what lay ahead, but he was ready and challenged to be useful to the Lord all the days of his life.

A life of adventure, no, many adventures lay ahead for Chuck Thomas. Come with me through these pages as I share with you the extraordinary life and vision of this man, and see how his missional life unfolded.

This book does more than chronicle the events of Chuck's life. It attempts to show the heart of a great man who used his time and talents for the Lord. His was a lifetime of service in obedience to God's call on his life. He made a difference. This book is also intended as a challenge for you to realize you, too, can make a difference. You, too, can live a missional life. You, too, can be used by God in unique ways yet to be discovered.

As you read on, I hope you can see Chuck Thomas as I do now, peering over the balcony of heaven, cheering you on to do the work the Lord has *just for you* in your time.

Chapter Two
DECISIONS COUNT

"My brothers and my sisters, listen up," shouted the preacher as he pounded the pulpit with his fist. "Right here in the Bible the apostle Paul tells us, 'Don't you know that you yourselves are God's temple and that God's Spirit lives in you? If anyone destroys God's temple, God will destroy him; for God's temple is sacred, and you,' my brothers and sisters 'are that temple.' There it is, as plain as day, written right there in your Bible in 1 Corinthians 3:16 and 17. You can't smoke tobacco and you can't contribute to this sin by growing tobacco. This too is a sin. This makes you a sinner. And a sinner making other people sin!"

W. F. Chappel, an evangelist, was holding a two-week meeting at the little, white building called The Saints Church in the remote hills of Kentucky. The farmers and country folk flocked to hear him, each night many of them making their way forward to the altar. His voice was resounding as he was totally involved in delivering his message. Preaching about tobacco, he had the full attention of these farmers.

"Look around you. Here you are in this part of Kentucky where everyone is growing tobacco. Does that make it all right for you to grow it? No! No! And NO! It is a sin to use it, and it is a sin to grow it because you are also your brother's keeper. Our bodies are the temple of God. Yes, God's temple."

Sitting halfway back was a young couple, Malcolm and Christeen Thomas, and her parents, Charlie and Lizzie Conyers. Christians, yes. They loved the Lord and went to church every service. They had never heard a message like this one. They were tobacco farmers. Everybody around there grew tobacco. That is how they put bread on their tables and clothes on their backs. Tobacco produced five times more money than any other crop. Tobacco was their livelihood. These two couples were shrinking in their seats. What were they supposed to do? There were only two more nights of this meeting with Bro. Chappel, but each evening around the supper table the conversation had turned to tobacco. What were they to do?

Back in those hills and hollows of Kentucky in the 1920s lay the small town of Carlisle, just west of the Lexington-Maysville pike. At the next crossroads was the village of Crayton, with the Conyers' General Store on the right and a couple of houses, the post office, and a blacksmith shop on the left. The First World War Treaty of Versailles had been signed in 1919, William Harding replaced Woodrow Wilson as president, and the United States was pretty much back to normal. And all the farmers grew the most lucrative crop, tobacco.

The next year when Bro. Chappel was back preaching at The Saints Church, the Thomas and Conyers families were there again every night. Actually, most of the people from up those hollows were there. News of the meeting had traveled all through the hills, and the people hitched up their buggies and headed to the church. It was the place to be.

That year, after praying about it and discussing the consequences, Malcolm and Christeen Thomas, her parents Charlie and Lizzie Conyers, and their daughters Liz and Hazel, all chose to obey the Lord. The next evening when Brother Chappel called for a decision for Christ, they all went forward and rededicated their lives to the Lord. They realized they had to make another decision, a decision about raising tobacco and obeying his command whatever the cost.

Gathered around the dining table together the next day, they searched for some options. What could they do to earn a living? Where should they go? Okay, if they left their farms, then what? A few weeks later they had a new idea. There was nothing around Crayton or Carlisle, but they had heard there were jobs available in the automobile factories in Dayton, Ohio. But that was too far away. Not one of them had ever been across the Ohio River, much less as far north as Dayton. How could they leave everything they had ever known and move to that distant land?

Then the patriarch of the family, Charlie Conyers, pulled out the Bible and read aloud where God had told Abram to go to a foreign country and he would go with him. On their knees, each one prayed for the Lord's direction. With a great deal of questions and anxious discussion, the decision was made. The Conyers would sell their General Store. Malcolm would relinquish his farm. And together they would leave their friends, their other relatives, and go on across the Ohio River to a land they didn't know in obedience to God's directive.

Playing with his blocks over in the corner of the room was three-year-old Charles Thomas, unaware that he had just escaped a life tied to tobacco into one of adventure led by the Lord, who had called his family to step out in faith and follow him.

Charles Franklin, aka "Charlie Francis"

Travel back with me three years before this moment in time to the world that welcomed Charles Franklin Thomas. We'll head there in an old Model T Ford, a bit noisy but quite popular at the time, down those winding roads among the hills and hollows of Kentucky.

The moon lights our way along the path as it continues to twist and turn through the hills. Except for the occasional dim light from small farmhouses that dot the landscape, it is quite dark as the moon slips behind the passing clouds on this night of September 28, 1923. Among the tobacco farms is one with a small log cabin partially hidden in the trees. A typical tobacco barn is close to the road, easy to see. All the farmers here have barns like this one to dry the tobacco leaves. We turn into the rutted drive approaching the cabin.

Tied to the porch post is a horse and buggy. Everyone around here knows that buggy. It belongs to the only doctor in these parts. Turning off our engine and listening closely, we hear the crying of a newborn, a little boy just arrived to bless this young dad and eighteen-year-old mom, Malcolm and Christeen Thomas.

Franklin Thomas (known as "Francis"), father of young Malcolm Thomas, is head of one of the leading families in the area and a man well thought of by the people of Nicholas County. As a tobacco farmer, he does quite well. His son Malcolm is following in his father's footsteps. He has acquired some land and is raising tobacco too. Just a little over a year before the birth of Charles Franklin Thomas, Malcolm married Christeen, the daughter of Charles (known as "Charlie") Conyers, the owner of Conyers' General Store. The doctor delivering this baby knows both sets of grandparents quite well, so when the baby arrives, Malcolm proudly tells the doctor he and Christeen are naming this first child after both of the grandfathers. The doctor writes the child's name on the birth certificate as "Charlie Francis Thomas," using both grandfathers' nicknames. Young Charles ("Chuck") is in grade school in Ohio before his parents manage to get another birth certificate with the intended name, Charles Franklin Thomas.

Kentucky Memories

A few years after we were married, Chuck Thomas took me down those winding roads to show me the old Franklin Thomas homestead and that part of Kentucky. As we drove by a house similar to the one his father Malcolm had owned, Chuck related stories of his six years growing up in the area. One of those stories was about the time his Aunt Elizabeth, who was only about six years old at the time, was asked to rock him to keep him from crying.

"She wrapped me up and put me in the rocking chair close to the fireplace," he said, "so I would keep warm. Liz, however, got a little aggressive with her rocking. She ended up rolling me out of the chair and right into the fireplace! Fortunately the fire had burned down, and she was able to stomp out the flames on my blanket. I was unharmed."

As we continued on those hilly roads, Chuck told another story about how the Lord had again protected him when he was just a baby. "Now that I remember this story, it tells me again that the Lord certainly had plans for me and protected me right here at the beginning of my life," he said.

There was a place about two miles on down the road where gypsies often came and camped. They traveled in caravans. When we would hear about them coming, Grandpa Conyers would lock all but one of the General Store doors and let only four or five in at a time so they didn't carry the store off. One day some gypsies came by our house, as they did occasionally. My mom told me she answered the door and a gypsy tried to sell her something. I was asleep in my crib in the other room. All of a sudden she heard a big commotion. Another one of the gypsies had crept in the back door and was gathering me up in my blanket to steal me.

My dad had a big bird dog at the time. You needed one out on the farm. He was very reliable and very obedient, a valuable dog but never allowed in the house. Sensing trouble, that dog burst through the screen door and attacked the gypsy. The gypsy dropped me back in my crib and ran out the door with the dog chasing him down the road. Although that dog had never been in the house before, somehow he'd sensed the danger. He was even more valuable after that day and became a prized blessing to our family.

Life in Ohio

Malcolm Thomas, Chuck Thomas's dad, moved his family to Ohio just as he had told the Lord he would. He landed a job with Delco Products, a division of General Motors. He and Christeen found a small house on the west side of Dayton and settled there. Through inquiry, they located the First Church of God at 3300 West Third Street. Young Chuck Thomas, then six years old, started the first grade. Shortly after that, a baby sister, Wilda Mae, joined the family. Life was going well for the Thomas family in this new place.

Charlie Conyers, Christeen's father, also moved his family as he told the Lord he would. He found a location in downtown Dayton and opened a clothing store, where he sold jeans and workers' clothing. He was a man who loved the Lord, and when he opened the doors of his store, he also opened his heart to help his customers. If he wasn't busy out front selling jeans or shoes, he was teaching the Bible to new friends in the back room. He didn't stop there. He was also feeding those who were hungry and giving clothes to those who were desperate. He named his place "The Lee Store" and featured Lee brand jeans.

Young Chuck Thomas was tall and lanky, and at age nine he became a paperboy. This job enabled him to buy a bicycle. His next job was at a grocery, where he cleaned the produce and arranged it for sale. As a teenager, he attended Roosevelt High School, where he played the violin in the orchestra and the trombone in the band. He enjoyed being a part of the band so much that he also became the drum major. He loved to twirl a baton as he led the high school band on parades through Dayton.

One year Chuck's band director discovered that the renowned trombonist Tommy Dorsey was coming with his band to play at Lakeside Pavilion. Dorsey had made an offer that the best trombonist in all the Dayton schools could play with him one night. Chuck tried out, and he was selected. He was ecstatic, but when he told his parents, they were not happy. The event was a public dance, not a church function, and they were "not happy."

Chuck really wanted to play with Dorsey's orchestra, so his band director helped him, even lending him the right clothes to wear. The clothes were much too big, as Chuck was a skinny kid, so it took several safety pins to keep the pants on. When the band played Dorsey's theme song, "I'm Getting Sentimental Over You," Chuck was given the honor of playing the solo part instead of Dorsey. Then, as Tommy Dorsey stepped forward, the band changed keys, moving the song a couple of steps higher. Dorsey played it again for the audience.

Chuck always felt honored that he had what he considered a wonderful opportunity to play with one of the big bands of that time. He had no idea how music would figure into his life in the years ahead.

The strong values of Chuck's parents and grandparents and pastor shaped him for a life of his own tough decisions. Chuck's father was always faithful at church, serving in any and every job given to him. His grandfather Conyers had a significant influence in his life, as he was always helping people at his store and leading them to the Lord. Chuck's pastor, Dale Oldham, was a strong source of encouragement during his army years. The faith and inspiration of those mentors helped shape the life and future that lay ahead for Chuck Thomas. At an early age, Chuck claimed Isaiah 30:21 as his own: "Whether you turn to the right or to the left, your ears will hear a voice behind you, saying, 'This is the way; walk in it.'"

Chapter Three
GREETINGS FROM UNCLE SAM!

"Hey, Chuck, come over here. Here's the letter you were expecting," said Chuck's dad, handing him a yellow envelope. Chuck stared at it for a second and then tore it open.

"Dad, this is it. It's my 'Greetings from Uncle Sam!' This is my call for induction. Well, we knew it would be coming ever since I turned eighteen and registered for the draft, and here it is now."

Yes, the draft for military service was still in effect. Since World War I, all young men had to sign up for it when they turned eighteen years old. In Chuck's hand was his call to serve his country. It was a frightening thought for an eighteen-year-old. The world was reeling with conflict in the late 1930s when Chuck was a teenager at Roosevelt High School in Dayton, Ohio. Hitler was in power in Germany, and with his Nazi troops, he was taking one country after another into his empire. Stalin had taken control of Russia and was turning it into a communist regime. Mussolini had Italy under his control and was looking to join forces with Hitler. Hirohito in Japan was expanding his territory and brutally taking over Korea, China, Hong Kong, the Philippines, and many other countries in Asia. Totalitarian dictators threatened to control much of the free world.

France had built the Maginot Line after WW I, but it didn't stop Hitler's forces from invading and occupying its land. By 1941, England was being bombed every night and expected an invasion at any time. United States President Franklin Roosevelt and Congress were taking the isolationist approach. They felt that, having both the Atlantic and the Pacific oceans to protect our nation, we could stay out of the bloodshed.

Then came Pearl Harbor, December 7, 1941. A shock to our nation. A day of infamy. Suddenly the United States had no choice. Like it or not, we were in the war. The country changed direction and focused intently on what it would take for the Allied forces to win the war against tyranny. Nothing was sure. The future of our country and the whole world was at risk. Men began joining the Army, Navy, and Marines in large numbers (the Air Force was part of the Army at that time). Women left their homes to work in factories to help our country build the planes, trucks, jeeps, weapons, bombs, and ammunition that would be needed. No more cars were manufactured. Gasoline was rationed. Tires were rationed. Food was rationed. Everything changed. Everything!

Everything and everybody were a part of the war effort. People were pulling together, doing whatever it took to protect their country, their homeland.

In the midst of this turmoil, Chuck graduated from high school in the spring of 1942, searched for a job, found one as an apprentice tool designer at Master Electric, and registered for the draft. On his birthday, September 28, 1942, he received his "greetings" and orders to report to Fort Thomas, Kentucky. It was just across the river from Cincinnati, and that was much better than he had expected.

Chuck's first assignment was with the Army band, and he liked that. He played his trombone. Stationed only fifty miles from Dayton, he was able to drive home almost every weekend. Tires were rationed, so when his began to wear out, he put newspapers inside between the tube and the outside rubber to be able to stay on the road. All was working fine until the Army changed Fort Thomas to a WAC (Women's Army Corp) base. The band was disbanded, and Chuck was moved to Fort McClellan, Alabama.

A Problem or an Opportunity?

Because of his religious convictions, Chuck had registered for service as a conscientious objector (CO), meaning that he would do anything but carry a gun and shoot people. His superior officer in Alabama didn't like his CO status and set out to change Chuck's mind. He was given the assignment of digging ditches in the hot Alabama summer sun. Other soldiers were given the same assignment but were on a rotation. Not Chuck. He was required to dig ditches and sweat in the heat of that southern sun every day.

Chuck understood that the assignment was given to him to test his character and commitment. He was challenged repeatedly by his superiors concerning his faith in God and his conviction not to kill anyone. They tried to talk him out of being a CO, kept at him continually, day and night, for what seemed forever to him. They worked hard to break him down, yet he stood firm. The Lord helped him have the right answer every time.

"Those times of being challenged as a conscientious objector were so hard," Chuck told me years later.

They would bring me into a room to question me, challenge me, and tell me I was a disgrace to my country. They had checked on the name of my sister, Wilda, and one time asked what I would do if the German soldiers came into our home and were going to kill Wilda and my mom and dad. Surely I would grab a gun and protect them. Surely I wouldn't just stand there and let them kill my family. These sessions put me on my knees. I had to pray and ask the Lord just what would he have me do. My answer to them was usually that the Lord would help me make the right decision at the right time, and I couldn't make that decision now.

The bad news is that this questioning went on repeatedly. The good news is that the Lord helped me through it all. My superiors finally gave up and placed me in the medical corp. What a relief that was. It certainly helped me learn to depend on the Lord for his answers and his guidance. Actually the experience taught me to depend on him, as I would need it even more in those foxholes in France, Holland, and Belgium later on.

Learning to depend on the Lord was new to me. I had a tremendous mentor in my father. I was blessed with significant influence of my grandfather Conyers as he demonstrated his values in always helping people at his store. I also had Dr. Dale Oldham, my pastor, who had confidence in me and I knew was praying for me. But now it was up to me to decide who I was and whom I would follow, come what may. Yes, learning to depend on the Lord and handle the challenges that were waiting for me became a new way of life for me. I was just beginning to realize how the Lord would lead me no matter what, no matter where.

After several months and losing a lot of weight because of the hard work he was assigned, Chuck was placed in the 35th Infantry Division Medical Corps as an ambulance driver and transferred to Fort Bragg, North Carolina. Next came the training. He learned how to be a medic and take care of the wounded and dying. He did the marches, the climbing cliffs and repelling, and learned how to maintain and repair his ambulance. All soldiers were getting ready for something major—the invasion of Europe.

On to the European Theater of Operations

In February of 1944, at age twenty, Chuck received his orders to sail to England to be a part of the European theater of operations. His unit was placed on a Liberty ship headed to Liverpool. While crossing the Atlantic, the ship had to dodge numerous German submarines. What would ordinarily have been a six- or seven-day voyage turned into twenty-eight days. He would later tell people that he was seasick twenty-nine of those twenty-eight days.

At this point, Hitler and his German army were winning. They had conquered Belgium, Holland, Denmark, and France and were fighting Russia in the east. His troops were strong. His forces moved forward relentlessly. Hitler was well on his way toward his goal of gaining control of England as well. General Eisenhower had been chosen as Allied Supreme Commander, and he was gearing up troops from England, America, and Australia to invade France and stop Hitler. He was moving several hundred thousand U.S. soldiers into England in preparation. Chuck was just another one of those soldiers, along with his ambulance. The Allied forces were getting ready for the big invasion—D-Day.

Bob Leis Remembers

Bob Leis is Chuck's cousin. Here is what he remembers about this time.

I have been very hesitant to put much on paper for a couple of reasons. First, I was a very young boy at the time and was not told what was happening. I believe that time is a good healer and that you forget many of the bad things that affect you and remember more of the good times, especially as a child. Second, the Dayton area was not a place where anyone did a lot of talking about the war. We had six divisions of General Motors manufacturing war products at full tilt: machine guns, bomb sights for Air Force bombers, parts for troop carriers and tanks, and ammunition shells (bullets). We also had NCR (National Cash Register Co.) heavily involved in developing code breakers for the German and Japanese codes. Nearby Miamisburg was the location of Mound Laboratories, which was a city built completely underground to develop all kinds of parts and theories for bombs, especially for a new bomb called an atomic bomb.

Then there was Wright Field and Patterson Field, which did most of the fighter and bomber designs and tests. I remember hearing strange-sounding airplane motors and running and hiding for fear that a German plane had gotten through and was coming to bomb Dayton. We were always told that if the Germans wanted to kill the most people, they would bomb New York City, but if they wanted to win the war, they would bomb Dayton.

We were told never to talk about the war, because maybe the person sitting next to you on the streetcar might be a German spy. Needless to say, security in Dayton was very, very high. I guess these were some of the reasons why you did not ask a lot of questions. Some people were arrested for simply asking too many questions.

Chapter Four
WORLD WAR II

It was time. World War II was escalating. Chuck and his unit arrived in Liverpool. Crossing the English Channel was ahead. Then the invasion of all invasions. At just twenty years of age, Chuck would be part of the deadliest conflict in human history and the most famous battle of World War II. His time among the bombs, the deafening noise of battle, the wounded and dying, more than any other time in his life before and after, shaped him for his calling. Here are some of Chuck's recollections from that time.

D-Day

June 6, 1944. It was D-Day, and I was scared. I knew we were going to invade Europe at Normandy in France, and I would be going in on Omaha Beach. I had been in England with the 35th Infantry Division, 110th Medical Battalion for a few months and had seen some of the countryside. The British were really under attack with the Nazi planes bombing London every single night. There was no assurance as to who was going to win this war. Hitler had it planned. He was going to rule the world. He was attacking with all his might. It was a wild and scary time. And Hitler was winning.

For the D-Day invasion, I had to prepare my ambulance to drive under about five feet of water. That meant extending the exhaust pipe upward and covering the spark plugs and electrical connections. Then they loaded us on a landing craft. One end of the craft would fold down so you would drive on or off that way. The landing craft was small and only held five vehicles. I drove mine on first and then realized I'd also be the first one to drive off into the water.

Late the night of June 5th, we headed across the English Channel from Southampton, England. The sky was completely filled with our warplanes. Ships were everywhere carrying soldiers, tanks, trucks, jeeps, and all kinds of equipment heading for Normandy. It was scary. I was really trembling and shaking. Then it came time for me to drive off into the water. It looked like miles from the shore. I started my engine. The front wheels dropped off the boat, and they seemed to go down forever until they finally hit the bottom of the ocean. I could hardly keep my hands on the steering wheel, as they were shaking so hard. Next, the back wheels dropped off, but the back of my ambulance floated. I managed to work my ambulance toward the land amid all the battle, the gunfire, the rockets, and the confusion. It was totally scary. I was praying all the time.

Finally coming to the shore, I saw bodies of fallen soldiers everywhere, and I had to drive around them. I got to a captured German bomb shelter and managed to get inside with many other U.S. troops. We stayed there for three days as the fighting continued. The noise was terrific, but we were safe inside. The bomb shelter, however, was so crowded that we all had to sleep practically standing up.

We spent a lot of time in Normandy. The fighting among the hedgerows was worse than I could imagine. I heard later it was much worse than Eisenhower had anticipated. The terrain was so difficult that we couldn't make any headway. We lost thousands of soldiers every day and made very little progress. It was weeks before we moved on down farther into France. When we finally did get out of the hedgerows, we made more progress. The fighting was bitter. One of the first towns we liberated was St. Lo.

At another time we were in a fierce battle. One of my buddies knew he was in trouble, so he yelled, "Tommy!" That's what they called me in the army. "Tommy," he cried out, "tell me about God, quick." There wasn't time for anything but a quick prayer. He died within minutes.

I was going from one soldier to another bandaging up wounds, applying medicine, and finding those I could take back to the aid station. It was shocking to see so many dying all around me. I had never seen death before. Stationed on the front lines, I was right in the middle of it.

Liberation of Paris

After the GI's liberated Paris in 1944 from Nazi aggression, I got a pass and went to see that famous city. How great it was to see the Opera House, the Eiffel Tower, the Arc of Triumph, and the Cathedral of Notre Dame. None of them had been damaged by the war. Paris is also the location of the tomb of Napoleon.

He was France's great military leader in the 1800s, conquering most of Europe before he died. The French built a special monument for his tomb, and inside the center was a lower area where the tomb itself was placed. That made it available to be viewed by looking down from the floor level. When I came to Napoleon's tomb, I jumped over the railing and stood on top of his tomb, raising my arms in a sign of victory. We, the GI's, were freeing France from the Nazis. We were the liberators. I felt triumphant.

Battle of the Bulge

The Battle of the Bulge was Hitler's last great offensive. Our forces were pushing him back into Germany, and he was beginning to realize he was losing the war. Deciding that the Allied forces' most vulnerable spot was in the Ardennes Forest, he sent in his strongest men and his best tanks to start an offensive, hoping to regain his position in the war. The battle was fierce. Thousands of soldiers were killed on both sides. It was awful and so bloody, plus it was the coldest January in decades. I was working hard to help the wounded and get them back to the aid station. It was dangerous, never knowing when a shell might come my way. I was treating the wounded and going from one to the other to see who I could help. If they were alive, I picked them up, put them in my ambulance, and headed back to the aid station. Our 35th Infantry lost one third of all our men in this one fight.

One time when I got to the aid station, the soldier I had brought had died on the way. The "Ole Man," that is what we called the doctor at the aid station, told me to put him over with the others that were dead and stacked just to the side. While I was doing that, a supply truck arrived and unloaded some new medicines. We had never seen these medicines until then, but back home work was underway to find new medicine to help our soldiers on the front lines. We had not had adrenaline. It was new. So the Ole Man told me to try it on one of those dead soldiers in the stack. I went to the one I had just brought in, pulled up his sleeve, and gave him a shot. That wasn't hard. Went back to see what else I should do before heading back to the front lines.

Before long, the soldier I had given the shot to started moaning and groaning. Wow! The Ole Man rushed over to him, and we carried him back inside to the examination table. He started working on him as he was coming around. Then the Ole Man told me to put him back in the ambulance and take him to the field hospital farther back so they could treat him and monitor him. I never knew who he was, but I sure would have liked to tell him later how close he came to dying. That new medicine saved his life.

Another new medicine was discovered at that time. Sulfa. It worked great, and we used it a lot. It seemed that the pharmaceutical laboratories were working hard to give us new medicines that we so desperately needed for all the sick and wounded.

In a couple of days, we were in Brussels. I had parked the ambulance and was walking close to the buildings for protection when all of a sudden a woman jumped out of a fourth-story window with a knife in her hand aimed right at me. Fortunately, she missed and fell on the cement instead of on me. That was a close one. She was trying to kill me.

Farther up, we came to the Moselle River. It was wide and with a strong current. German troops were on the east bank ready to destroy us. We were sure the bridge was wired with explosives. We had to get across the river some way in order to win the war. The railroad bridge was still there, but again, we were afraid to use it. It would be detonated. We used pontoons and made our own bridge, even during the gunfire, and then drove the tanks, trucks, jeeps, and ambulances over. The fighting was fierce. Bloody. Seemed like the whole river turned red with blood. It was a bloody battle, but we finally got across and won the battle.

The Battle of the Bulge was very bloody. We lost thousands of soldiers, but praise the Lord, we won that battle. In the middle of it, our commander, General McAuliffe, was asked by Hitler to surrender. His reply was simply, "Nuts." I have a plaque with his name and "Nuts" on it.

The Winter of 1944–45

We had to dig foxholes to sleep in. Each of us would dig a hole big enough to crawl down into so we could sleep without being hit by bullets. Why a hole? The enemy would have a harder time shooting us in a hole. It was safer. The back of the ambulance would be better and a bit warmer, but it was too vulnerable to enemy fire.

That winter of 1944–45 was extremely cold. There were weeks at zero or below and lots of snow. We were out in it twenty-four hours a day with no place to go. We would wear all the clothes they had given us and all the socks we had. Our feet were so cold. Many of the soldiers lost a toe or foot by freezing. We had to eat our C-rations cold, as we could not build a fire because the enemy could locate it. It was bitter cold. I have never experienced anything like it or ever been as miserable as that winter.

I remember one time when I had dug a foxhole where I was going to spend the night. The ground was hard, and it was really difficult to dig that hole. After I had it about ready, I got a feeling that it wasn't right. I think the Lord was telling me that. It was hard work to dig that foxhole, and I didn't want to do it again, but I felt it was in the wrong place. I moved to a different area, managed to dig another one, and crawled in it. Sure enough, during the shelling that night, that first foxhole had a direct hit. If I had stayed in it, I would have been killed. This was another time when the Lord took care of me and saved my life.

One time I had three soldier buddies sitting with me by my ambulance. Suddenly bullets started coming, and all three were hit and killed. My ambulance took a direct mortar hit, and these men I had picked up to take to the aid station were killed, yet God spared my life even though I was wounded. Shrapnel from the explosion had gotten my right foot. I had to find my own way back to the aid station. Arriving there, I knew they would automatically cut off the rest of my foot. They didn't have time to fix up everyone. However, because I was part of their medical team, they worked on my foot so that it could be saved. Then I was sent farther back to the field hospital. That is how I got my Purple Heart.

One day before they evacuated me to England, I was sitting in front of the hospital in the sunshine. A German sniper sneaked through the lines and took a shot at me. The bullet lodged in the back of my chair just fractions of an inch from my head. Our guards immediately eliminated the sniper before any more shots could be made. These kinds of experiences made me know that the Lord was hearing my prayers and protecting me. Through all this I knew that when I returned home, I was to work for him and respond to his call to the ministry. He had a purpose for my life.

In a couple of days I was evacuated to a hospital in England for recuperation for a few months. That gave me more time to think about the protection the Lord had for me and consider what he had for me when I would get back home. In a month, I was hobbling around and well enough to head back to the front lines.

The War's End

After the Ardennes campaign, we crossed the Ruhr River and the Siegfried line in less than a week. We had liberated France, Holland, and Belgium and were in Germany. Winning the Battle of the Bulge was decisive. We knew we were going to win the war. We didn't know when, and we didn't know how many more of our men would be killed, but we were moving fast.

By March 11th we were at the Rhine River moving on to the Elbe River, close to Berlin. The Germans were retreating. Gross evidence of their cruelty and total disregard for people as human beings was all around us. These scenes were hard on me. Unbelievable. One time as we were driving in no-man's-land, there was a horrible odor. We came across a huge barn that had been packed with several hundred people and then set on fire. After the fire had died down, several German soldiers came back asking if anyone needed help. Those that responded were immediately shot. One man survived because he was hidden under a pile of bodies. He was the man who revealed the story of what had happened. This was hard to comprehend. It was heart wrenching. Impossible, but real. The smell was awful, but the idea, the fact they had burned all those people, was inconceivable.

Finally, finally, at last, the end of the war. The Germans laid down their guns, raised their hands, and surrendered. Unbelievable. Unimaginable. It was over. From D-Day, June 6, 1944, to VE Day, Victory in Europe, May 8, 1945, had been like an eternity.

Hitler had committed suicide. His forces had collapsed. No more war, no more fighting. I could go home.

We got our orders to turn around and head back toward France and the coast. It was a long trip, and so very different this time. We were met by people yelling, waving, and excited. The war was over, and they were not under the control of the Nazis any longer. It was victory. When I finally got to the coast, the military there took one look at my ambulance and decided it was junk. It was sunk in the Atlantic along with other useless vehicles.

Of my battalion of medics that went in, only ten of us went home at the end of the war. We went back to England, and in August were on board that majestic *Queen Mary* for the trip home. It was filled with GI's and a jubilant spirit. We were actually going home. On September 10, 1945, we came into New York harbor, passing by the Statue of Liberty. What a beautiful sight. Then finally I was on a train for Indianapolis and Fort Benjamin Harrison to be mustered out. I had been in the service for thirty-three months, and I was actually going home.

I called my folks at the first chance, telling them I would be coming to Dayton on the Pennsylvania Railroad. The extended family, my grandparents, aunts, uncles, cousins, and of course Mom and Dad were at Union Station waiting for me. By then, my little sister had grown so much that I didn't recognize her. Home, 146 Reisinger Avenue, Dayton, Ohio, on September 13, 1945.

This was a time that I had sometimes thought would never arrive. Actually coming home again, and in one piece, something I often thought was impossible. And it was, except that the Lord had cared for me through it all. Through all the shells, the artillery, the bombs, the cold, the below freezing weather, the lack of food, the horrors of war, everything—my heavenly Father cared for me and brought me safely home.

Reliving Those Times

Those experiences overseas were used by God to help Chuck find his purpose and service to the Lord. He would often relive some incident of those experiences, sometimes using his stories to help others. Here are two examples in his words.

An amazing sequel to the Moselle River battle happened when Donna and I were in Brazil visiting churches in 1966. We had traveled to Rondon for a camp meeting of the German congregations in that area. Many Germans had migrated to Brazil after the war to start life over. One of the leading pastors was Brother Ruben Malzon. He had ridden a bus twenty-four hours from Curitiba to Rondon to be with us. We started talking about the war and discovered that he was in the same battle at the Moselle River, only he was on the other side, the German side. It was a victory that we had the opportunity to meet each other. We had that dangerous battle in common, and we both came out alive. We were both survivors and both believers in the Lord Jesus Christ. It was great to know him and to talk together about our common encounter and how our Lord took care of us through the battle. We were brothers now.

There is also a story about a little village in France that Donna and I drove to in 1978. It was a quiet and peaceful Sunday morning. We drove slowly down the main street so I could tell her about this village. My battalion had come upon it after one of our battles, and since no one was there, we could stay inside a house instead of outside in the cold winter of 1944–45. I said, "Donna, do you see that house? We slept there. First time inside in a long time, and it was so much better and warmer than any foxhole. See that house over there?" I pointed to another one. "That is where we did some cooking. We actually found some potatoes in their cellar and made French fries. Lots of them. They were so delicious and so much better than the cold C-rations we had all the time.

"When it was time to move forward, we were headed to go through that field you see there by those trees. About that time, some pigs got loose and ran in that direction looking for something to eat. All of a sudden, there was what seemed like hundreds of explosions. That field had been mined, and those pigs were stepping on the mines and being blown to bits. They certainly changed our plans. Those pigs saved our lives. We detoured around that field and went on down to the creek on the other side, then across that way, and on."

Learning to Depend on God

Chuck was just eighteen years old when he was drafted, and he was twenty-one when he returned home that September of 1945. Those were formative years in his life. All the trauma of D-Day, being on the front lines until the end of the war, caring for the dying and wounded, living in foxholes, combating the extreme cold, and the constant fear made the Chuck Thomas who returned home a man, a different man. He had learned to depend on God each and every moment. He had seen the frailty of life, which caused him to consider the purpose of his own life. Those foxholes, the whines of the bullets, and the bombs falling in front of him and behind him gave him a new sense of direction. He could tell others about the numerous times that the Lord had protected him. He felt confident that God had something special for him to do. He was ready to find his orders from his new commander-in-chief, God Almighty. In his heart he knew he was to be a minister for the Lord, get the message of the gospel to everyone he could, and be involved in saving people's lives versus watching them die in battle.

Chuck was ready for a change. He was ready to start the process of learning about ministry. He was ready to move on, looking at college, dreaming of planting a church, helping people find that precious relationship with the Lord, and hoping somewhere in the process that the Lord would give him a wife and a family. Dreams. Dreams that came out of those dark, traumatic times on the front lines.

Bob Leis Remembers

Chuck's cousin Bob Leis spent time with Chuck in the early days after he came home. His recollections are helpful in understanding what the aftermath was like for our soldiers. Bob was one of the first people to hear from Chuck that he intended to go into the ministry. Here are some of his memories.

> When Bud (that is what I always called him) came home at the end of the war, he was just a shell of the person that he had been when he left. He came to Grandma Conyers' house, and they set a bed up in the sitting room (nowadays better known as the family room). I remember him talking and screaming in his sleep. When he would wake up, he would just sit and tremble from head to foot until he would fall back to sleep again. After a couple of months, he started to calm down and act more like my Bud.

Suddenly, one day he announced that he was going to Anderson College to study for the ministry. I was disappointed and asked why he would leave us again. He told me that he hoped that I would never have to experience all the killing that he had seen on the battlefield. That he had promised God that if he came through it alive, he would do anything God wanted him to do. He explained how he drove an ambulance and that he had been a conscientious objector and that he always had an armed soldier with him sitting right next to him in the front seat. My memory is that three armed soldiers were killed while riding with him. Two ambulances took direct mortar hits, and everyone including the injured he was carrying was killed, yet God spared his life. All these memories were then flooding his total being. He wasn't the same, but he was home.

Experiences Count

The man I married, this Chuck Thomas, had indeed learned to depend on the Lord. As he would relate his war stories to me, his voice would be filled with emotion. He expressed unutterable appreciation for the way the Lord cared for him, from his first day in the Army, during those hard months digging ditches in the heat of Alabama, during the fear of a German submarine sinking the ship he was on while crossing the Atlantic to England, during that horrific experience of D-Day and all that followed it, during the continual dodging bullets across Europe, during the pain of so many dying as he was carrying them in his arms, and during the extreme cold of the winter of 1944–45

As I listened to Chuck, he taught me to thank the Lord in a new way as to how our heavenly Father orders our steps, cares of us in times like he would tell about, and gives us hope for the future that he has waiting especially for us. And what a future he had for Chuck. Read on, it gets exciting.

Chapter Five
COLLEGE YEARS

"Hey Chuck, what's this I hear about you going to Anderson College?"

"Yeah, pastor, that's where I'm going. I feel this is the next step the Lord has for me. He didn't get me out of those foxholes in Europe for nothing."

Chuck Thomas was one of the thousands of veterans around the nation who took immediate advantage of the college tuition benefit provisions of the GI Bill of Rights passed by Congress in June of 1944. As soon as he was mustered out of service and learned of the GI Bill, Chuck applied and was accepted at Anderson College, a small Christian college established by the Church of God in central Indiana. In January of 1946, Chuck traveled from his home in Dayton, Ohio, to the campus in Anderson, Indiana, to begin his first semester of college.

Chuck had been told by Joe, a family friend, about a girl from Tulsa he should look up at Anderson. Joe had met her during the summer when he visited her church in Oklahoma, and he had learned that she had enrolled at Anderson College for September of 1945. One day as Chuck was at the mailboxes, he heard the switchboard operator call across the room, "Hey, Donna! Donna Stanley! Come over here. I have something for you."

Chuck caught that name and remembered it as the same one that his family friend had mentioned. Turning his head, he saw this girl whose name he had heard only once before. This 6′ 2″, 165-pound young man with soft brown eyes and thick, dark hair immediately walked across the lobby to introduce himself to me. He mentioned the name Joe Hooker, our mutual friend who worked for NCR (National Cash Register) in Dayton and had been sent to Tulsa in 1945 to do some work there. Joe had attended the Church of God during those weeks he was in Tulsa, and I had met him during that time. When Joe learned I would be attending Anderson College in the fall, he told me about a GI from Dayton he thought was planning also to attend and said I should look him up. Chuck and I spent a few minutes in the mailroom chatting about Joe. He then stated that he wanted to spend some more time with me.

One day not long after that first meeting, as I was coming out of Old Main (the college administration building then), Chuck was standing there waiting. He greeted me and then said, "Donna, I have been asked to play my trombone for the Rotary Club next Tuesday. Would you accompany me on the piano?"

"Depends on what you are going to play," I replied.

"I think they would like 'The Love of God.' Will that work?"

"Yes," I replied, pleased that this young man had made yet another effort to connect with me.

Chuck really surprised me when he came to pick me up. He had a gift for me, a beautiful corsage of red roses. He impressed me. The evening worked so well so that we began to have more dates but without the trombone or the roses.

Healing of Memories

I soon learned that Chuck had a major problem. He was still an emotional wreck from the combat fatigue and stress of the war. He was scarred by war and the horrible memories of it. He couldn't sleep. He had nightly terror attacks. Too many battles going over and over through his mind. He was remembering too many soldiers dying in his arms. He told me he was still feeling the bullets whining by his head, still hearing the roar of the guns, still reliving all of those scenes, all those calls for help. He needed help. Somehow he had to overcome the trauma of those months of combat on the front lines.

He had been invited to join one of the campus men's clubs, so he chose the Booster Club. Other GI's were members, and he enjoyed their companionship. One weekend the Booster Club held an all-night prayer meeting for students on campus. Chuck volunteered to serve during the 3 a.m. to 4 a.m. slot, thinking that no one would come at that time and it would be the easiest.

About 3:15 that morning, as Chuck was alone, the door at the back of the building where the meeting was being held opened, and in walked the four top leaders of the college: President John Morrison; Dean Russell Olt; Dr. Carl Kardatzke, head of the education and psychology departments; and Dr. Adam Miller, Dean of Men. They told him that they had come to pray for him. They had heard how the trauma of the war was affecting every aspect of his life. Chuck shared with them how desperately he needed healing, and then these men of God prayed with him, asking the Lord to heal him of his combat fatigue. As they were leaving, Dr. Kardatzke turned to Chuck and asked him to come to his office later that day. He said he wanted to talk with him.

That afternoon Chuck went to Old Main and located Dr. Kardatzke's office. Dr. Kardatzke was waiting for him. "Charles," he said, "I want you to get pen and paper and write down everything you can remember about the war—all the attacks, the Normandy invasion, those times your buddies were killed, when you were wounded both times, and everything else you can think of that is troubling you. Write it all down, and bring it to me."

Chuck walked out of the office confused. He certainly didn't want to do that. Those memories hurt too much. He had been trying to forget them, and he had just been told to write about each one. No way. Yet he knew he had to respect Dr. Kardatzke for his desire to help him and to trust him that this step might help.

That night Chuck struggled to write about his memories and chose to write general memories as to what went on during the war. The next day he took his writings to Dr. Kardatzke, who studied them carefully and then said, "Charles, I think you have more memories than these. More personal memories. Take these back and work on them again. I want you to write down all the things you have left out. Everything that happened to you. I know this will be difficult, but it is a part of your healing process."

This assignment seemed too difficult for Chuck. Too painful. No, he didn't want to relive any of that. Months of battles, tens of thousands of men dying, many dying right in his arms, picking up the wounded, stacking up the dead, dodging bullets, bombs falling in front and behind, machine guns firing and piercing his ears, bitter cold, only C-rations to eat, snow and more deep snow, crossing rivers with his buddies dying on the right and on the left, rain, heat, bugs, and unsanitary conditions. Those were only a part of the memories. How could he comply with Dr. Kardatzke's instructions? How could he get out of this assignment? Those memories needed to be buried, he thought, not relived. Yet he could not find any other way to respond. He finally found his desk, asked the Lord to help him do what he knew he had to do, wiped his eyes, and started writing those horrible experiences, the things he desperately wanted to forget.

When Chuck went back to Dr. Kardatzke with what he had written the second time, Dr. Kardatzke again studied them intently. "Charles, this is better but I believe there are still more. There are encounters that you don't want to remember. Take what you have done back, and write everything you can possibly remember. Everything! Don't leave anything out. Search your mind, and write down all the pain, all the trauma, all the fear, all the hurts—everything."

As Chuck went back to his room, compelled to think of the trauma, the pain, the guns, and the dead, more encounters came to his mind. Things he had buried but they were still there. After some time in prayer, he chose to tackle the task and again picked up his pen. That time he wrote far more than he had the first two times.

The following day Chuck asked me to go with him to see Dr. Kardatzke, saying he needed some support. He didn't want to do it alone. I agreed to go with him but told him he needed to go into the office alone when we arrived. He came to my dorm for me and then dragged himself across the campus, up the stairs of Old Main, and knocked on Dr. Kardatzke's door. His secretary opened the door and directed him into Dr. Kardatzke's office. With relief Chuck handed him the papers, wanting to get out of there as quickly as possible. Once again Dr. Kardatzke looked them over carefully. Turning to Chuck, he said, "Are you sure this is all? Did you leave anything out?"

Chuck was getting upset. He had been compliant and done what he had been told, not once but three times. The trauma of reliving all those horrible memories and then having to express them on paper was excruciating. "Dr. Kardatzke, this is it, all of them," Chuck told him defiantly. "I've done what you asked. It was terrible to write these. It was difficult, really difficult to have to remember and write about all those times I was in battles, but everything you asked for is here. Everything!"

Dr. Kardatzke held Chuck's papers in his hands. Looking Chuck right in the eye, he took the papers and tore them in half, then again, and then again. He tore them up completely while Chuck watched, and then he threw them in his wastebasket.

"What he did was disgusting," Chuck told me when he came out. "As I watched, I was thinking, why did I go to all that trouble just to have him tear it to shreds? I am totally drained and confused."

Then came the amazing answer to the prayers of the president, the dean, Dr. Miller, and Dr. Kardatzke. After the shredding of all those stories that day, Chuck was able to sleep in peace for the first time in many months. He was changed. He was healed of his trauma. He was a new man. He was able to deal with the past, comfortable at last with being able to talk about it. Those who knew him praised the Lord for his deliverance. Chuck Thomas was now free to move into the future, the future God had waiting for him.

Marriage

In June of 1946, Chuck asked me to marry him. I was about to have the final exam in my Bible class in just an hour, so I told him to wait for my answer until it was over. He waited. When we got back together, I said yes, I would marry him. We agreed that he had to go to Tulsa to meet my parents and get their permission before our engagement could be made public.

We communicated that summer by mail. Every day Chuck sent me a letter. Each letter said the same thing: "I love you." He knew what he wanted and what God wanted him to do. His determination to serve the Lord enabled me to accept his plans for our future.

In August, Chuck took the New York Central and then the Frisco train out to Tulsa. My mom, dad, and brother went with me to the train station to welcome him. Two days later, Chuck approached my dad as he was milking his cow in the barn. Chuck cleared his throat and began, "Mr. Stanley, I would like to ask for your daughter's hand."

Dad was great on jokes, and he was expecting this moment. He looked up said, "My stars, Chuck. What do you want with another hand?"

"Well, I mean, I would like to have Donna as the mother of my children."

"What?" Dad was purposely making this moment funny and memorable. "How many children do you have?"

"No, no, no. I just mean I want to marry her. I don't have any children, but I want to marry Donna, and I need your permission."

After Dad quit laughing, he told Chuck that it would be fine. He didn't have any problem with our being married.

With Dad's endorsement, we started working on our wedding plans. The wedding ceremony would be in June of 1947. We had to put it off that long, as it was already August of 1946, and students were not allowed to marry during the school year. Classes lasted until the first week of June, so we set the date for June 12. The location would be the First Church of God, Tulsa, Oklahoma. Chuck asked Joe Hooker to be best man, since he had been the one who arranged for us to meet. My brother, Charles Stanley, was a pianist, so he would play the wedding music. Chuck's sister, Wilda, sang in church, so she would be the soloist. We added a couple of bridesmaids and groomsmen plus my two younger cousins for flower girls. That was our wedding party.

On June 10, 1947, Chuck's mom and sister traveled to Tulsa with Chuck on the New York Central and the Frisco trains. His dad couldn't get off work. Neither his mother nor sister had ever done anything like that or been that far from home before. The wedding ceremony was wonderful. Both of us felt we were living a dream. The reception was at my parent's house at 6539 South Lewis in Tulsa. It was supposed to be in the backyard, but some rain sprinkles moved it inside to the big back porch.

Chuck didn't have a car, so two days later my parents drove us to the little crossroads of Branson, Missouri, where we were to take a ferry on to Lake Taneycomo, the location Chuck had chosen for our honeymoon. After a few days in Lake Taneycomo, we caught the bus to Springfield, Missouri, and then the train back to Anderson.

Home in Indiana

Chuck Thomas had already made a decision that he wasn't going to pay rent. He did, however, have to rent an apartment from another college couple for us to live in for our first two months that summer. He wanted to build a house for us. His friend Simon Robinson liked his idea too, so they purchased two lots less than a mile from the college for $300 each. They were located at 2211 and 2215 East 6th street in Anderson. Of course, that part of Anderson was not what it is today. It was on the edge of town with no big streets or thoroughfares anywhere around. Sixth Street was only a dirt road. But it was close enough to the college to serve our purpose.

The next step was to find a house plan we liked. Looking through some catalogs with all kinds of plans, we picked one because the picture of it was so attractive. It wasn't a wise choice for a novice carpenter because it had an upstairs, but it did show a pretty yard with flowers. The house we chose had two bedrooms, a kitchen, a laundry, a living room with dining area, and one bath. Chuck secured a loan for $3,500 and started the project. He had never built anything before, but he didn't choose to ask why he should do something like this but instead, why not. It was exciting and quite different from anything either of us had experienced, to build a house, to try something we had never done before. Chuck was always seeing challenges and accepting them. His way of seeing life was becoming the way we would live.

By September, he had the roof on and the frame in good shape. The siding was on. No windows or doors were in yet, but it was time to move out of the apartment, so we did. We had no furniture either. We went to the junkyard and found a set of bedsprings, brought them home and covered them with blankets. That was our bed. We found more junk furniture and moved it in. The bathroom wasn't finished, but we had a path in the backyard to a makeshift outhouse. It worked. Chuck had the furnace of our house working by Easter (after a cold Indiana winter). We learned how to keep the kitchen warm and do our studying at college. Until the walls were plastered, we could read "This side up" on each sheet of insulation in every room.

Besides being full-time students those next three years and building our house, Chuck and I both worked part-time at East Side Jersey Dairy in food service. Chuck was the assistant manager. He made 90 cents an hour. I cooked hamburgers and waited tables for 50 cents an hour. Chuck seemed to enjoy every minute of it. Working there also provided some of our meals too. Chuck's mom thought we had lost our minds. When his parents came over from Dayton to visit us, she would cry when they drove off. They had given us an electric kitchen stove for a wedding present, and she did realize that was what was keeping us warm. Chuck's dad understood his son's spirit, and he encouraged him every chance he had. Because of the distance between Tulsa and Anderson, my folks only came up once a year to see us, and that was in June to attend Anderson Camp Meeting. Each year they could see the progress Chuck had made and were pleased with his ability to take care of their daughter.

Since Chuck had been delivered from the trauma of the war and was able to share his experiences with others, he was asked to go to various Youth for Christ rallies to tell his war stories and play his trombone. He loved to do that. He counted it a privilege to tell how the Lord had protected and delivered him. Audiences were eager to hear his stories. He was one of the few veterans who could and would tell their stories. So many others had not had the blessing of being released from the trauma of their war memories as he had.

First Flights into Ministry

Chuck became intrigued with the idea of flying. He found the opportunity to join a flying club and take lessons. The Piper Cub was as small a plane as one could get for training at the time, but it served his purpose. He was able to get his pilot license by learning to fly it. Little did he know how much this step would influence him later in his ministry.

One of the fun things Chuck did during our college years was to start a band for the college. They didn't have one, and they did have exciting times at the basketball games. Pulling together his friends on campus that played an instrument, he immediately had a band—not a big one, not an accomplished one, but one to add a great amount of enthusiasm for the basketball team. In a couple of years, the music department accepted the challenge.

In his senior year of college, Chuck became president of the Booster Club, which offered him many opportunities to serve and many friends. The coursework for his Bible major and graduation was nearly completed, so he applied for ordination with the Ohio Assembly of the Church of God. The committee approved him for ordination, and for their December meeting we drove to Columbus, Ohio. It was certainly a memorable time for us, since in our eyes all the important preachers were there. At last he really was a preacher—well, almost. He was still learning how to preach, but he was ordained.

Chuck's first sermon after ordination was in a church in Winchester, Indiana, a stone's throw from Anderson. He put a lot of work into that message, and it lasted all of ten minutes. At that time, college professors really didn't teach students how to preach, so it was trial and error. Chuck kept working on improving his sermons, and soon he became an excellent preacher.

After his ordination, he filled in regularly to preach at a church in the Over-the-Rhine area of Cincinnati, Ohio, on weekends. It was an eye-opening experience. The church was in the inner city, and it ministered to people very different from who we were. The storefront building used for services simply had a sign out front calling it a church. The piano was a bit of a problem. It was so flat that Chuck had me play the songs in sharps on the piano while he played them in flats on his trombone in order to put us on the same tone. It wasn't exactly easy, but it worked. Chuck would preach both Sunday morning and evening, and then we would head back to Anderson.

During spring break in 1948, Jim Holder, pastor of a church near Liberal, Kansas, asked Chuck to come and hold a youth revival. This invitation excited him, so off he went, trombone in hand. He took the train, as it was the best form of transportation at that time for us. Near the end of his week there, a heavy rain came. On Sunday afternoon with more bad weather predicted, Pastor Holder decided to cancel the evening service. He took Chuck to the station for an earlier train than had been planned, exchanged his ticket, and put him on board. Chuck was on his way back to Anderson.

An hour later, the call came for all ministers in that part of Kansas to come and assist with a train wreck caused by the storm. The eight inches of rain that had fallen during the afternoon caused a bridge to give way, dumping the evening train into the river. Six persons were killed and almost one hundred were injured, some very seriously. The scene of the accident was just forty miles east of Liberal, so Pastor Holder responded to help the injured. Working his way down the aisle of the wrecked train, he came across the very seat Chuck had been assigned to occupy before his ticket was changed for a seat on the afternoon train. The passenger in the seat was dead. Once again God had protected Chuck from death.

Chuck had started college a semester after I did, which enabled me to get my B.A. degree in June and a job in September. I found a job teaching first and second grades in Lapel, Indiana. We took my total earnings of $2,400 that year and bought a brand new, beautiful, blue Buick. It replaced the Plymouth coupe Chuck had purchased for us from the junkyard shortly after we were married. It had given us so much trouble. A certain policeman kept us in his sight and stopped us repeatedly to kick the tires. He suggested we get that "rattletrap" off the road. When we began driving a big, new Buick, he just waved us on with a smile.

Chuck graduated in 1950 with his B.S. degree in Bible and education. We were able to finish the house and put it on the market two months before his graduation. It sold very quickly for $8,500. He had made a good decision in building that house. It was a good investment and a great experience. We had $2,000 in our pockets as we left college to go to Wichita, Kansas, where Chuck would begin his first pastorate. The last of June of 1950, we pulled out of our driveway in our new Buick, pulling a little trailer with all our earthly possessions, heading west to Kansas. A new adventure was ahead. A step forward in obedience to the Lord's call to Chuck that he had heard so distinctly in those foxholes in Europe. Chuck was going to be the associate pastor for Rev. Elmer Kardatzke, known to him as Uncle Mit, at the First Church of God. This Rev. Kardatzke was one of the clan of nine Kardatzke's from Elmore, Ohio, making him the brother to Dr. Carl Kardatzke who had helped Chuck overcome his combat fatigue from the front lines of the war.

Yes, it was time to move forward. Putting all our possessions in a little two-wheel trailer, we headed west. What was ahead? What would it be like for Chuck to be a pastor? He was looking forward to becoming an active, missional disciple of the Lord. How would his life unfold?

Chapter Six
GO WEST, YOUNG MAN

That old saying, "Go west, young man," was what Chuck was thinking as we headed for a new life in Kansas. He was praying, "Okay, Lord, what do you have ahead for us? Where do we start? How do we do this? Here we are. Use us and help us do what you want us to do."

First Assignment: Camp Fellowship

Chuck's first assignment was to be the summer caretaker of a church camp, located twenty miles west of Wichita on Lake Afton. He was challenged by the job, and summer can be HOT in Kansas. Our lodging was a small cottage by the lake. We managed to get through many 100-degree days and nights and still stay healthy. This camp, Camp Fellowship, was also where the Kansas churches in the Church of God affiliation had their annual Camp Meeting each August. Camp Meeting in those days was a time for pastors and all Christians to come together for a week of preaching, learning, recreation, and fellowship. Most of them brought their whole family and tents or trailers for their lodging. Almost all of the Kansas Church of God pastors came to Camp Meeting, so Chuck used this time as an opportunity to get acquainted with many of them.

The camp caretaker duties were basically 24/7. Though Chuck was busy all summer with the various dorms and cabins, the dining Quonset hut (Quonset huts were built during WWII as temporary corrugated metal army buildings prefabricated and built with a circular arching roof to serve as simple shelters because other building materials were scarce at that time) and its upkeep and production, the chapel with its equipment, plus the grass, the weeds, and especially the swimming pool, he did make time to search for a place for us to live after the camp assignment. Chuck was always looking ahead, preparing for what was next.

In August Chuck found a new and suitable house that he thought would be just right for us on the southeast side of Wichita, at 2103 Hodson, right beside the canal. He could buy it through a provision of the GI Bill. This brand new, three-bedroom frame house seemed great, and we were able to close the deal and move right in. It was easy to move in, as we only had the stove and refrigerator we had brought from Anderson. So we had to scramble to locate second-hand stores and discount shops to find a bed, couch, table, chairs and all that would help make this house our home.

A Pastor and a Music Teacher

In September Chuck checked in with the pastor at the First Church of God on South Market Street. He was ready to start the position as associate pastor, which is what had brought us to Wichita. The morning of the meeting, Chuck anxiously headed for the church office to talk with Rev. K. (Kardatzke) and find out what his duties would be. Chuck opened the conversation.

"Brother K., I am excited about being your associate. It will be great. I am really looking forward to getting started."

"I'm glad you are here too, Chuck," responded the pastor, "and I have been looking forward to having you. How did you like Camp Fellowship? Was it a good time out there?"

"Oh, it was super and just right to meet so many people," Chuck replied, "but now I am ready to get into the business of being a pastor. When do I start, and what do you want me to do?"

"You can start today, Chuck, but I need to tell you that the church doesn't have any funds for your salary. I will personally give you $10 a week, and maybe that will help." The pastor looked Chuck in the eyes and waited for a response.

This news was completely unexpected, a big surprise. He'd expected a salary, but Chuck wasn't going to let that stop him. Since he had chosen to move to Wichita to begin his ministry, he still wanted to be the associate pastor. He lived on the premise that if one door was closed, he must go find another one. The challenge for financial support sent us scrambling for an additional source of income. Fortunately we were both able to get jobs teaching school, and he was also able to start immediately as the associate pastor.

Chuck was hired at Eureka Junior High School to teach music. He soon discovered the school had never had a band. He wanted to know why, and then as was his nature, he felt the challenge to start one. Why not? It was a lot of work. During those two years Chuck was there as a teacher, he taught everything from drums to trumpets. Of course, the students really liked it. They were so excited about a band, their own band. They would do anything for him.

Chuck was learning to see opportunities ahead and was always ready to accept a challenge. During his time at Eureka, the Lord gave

Chuck another challenge. The school was in a distressed area of Wichita. Seeing the needs of the students, he decided to start a "gathering" on Thursday nights in the school gym. Why not? The students were his kids, and they needed this opportunity to connect with each other in a safe environment. He would have them play games for a while, and then he would lead them in discussions and songs that opened the door for him to share Christ and his message. These students had never had anything quite like this before. They brought their friends and more friends until Chuck had quite a large group. It was so successful that many of the kids came to him years later, after they had graduated from high school, to have him perform their wedding ceremony.

Chuck's work as a teacher was a full-time job, but his priority was still being a pastor. In his part-time job as associate pastor of First Church of God, Chuck was able to work with the senior high and college youth, teach Sunday school, make hospital calls, preach about once a month, and often lead in worship.

Planting a Church: Pawnee Avenue Church of God

Chuck's heart desire was to pastor a church full-time. It was what he knew the Lord had called him to do while he was in those foxholes in Belgium and France. So after a year as associate pastor at First Church of God, he was ready to find a full-time pastorate. Pastor Kardatzke had a different idea.

"Chuck, would you consider starting a church here in Wichita? I think there are lots of opportunities for a church on the east side of town. We could help you do that this next year."

Another challenge. It sounded exciting, and Chuck certainly wanted to get into a full-time pastorate. Why not?

He looked at areas of the city to find what land might be available. He found a couple of acres on Pawnee Avenue. It was actually close to McConnell Air Force Base and the Boeing and Cessna aircraft factories. With all the people working there, it seemed to be a great location. The plans were drawn, fund soliciting began, and construction started. Men from First Church came over in the evenings and Saturdays to do the hundreds of odd jobs that went along with the construction.

September 7, 1952, the Pawnee Avenue Church of God building was dedicated. The sanctuary could hold up to 250 people, and it was completely full that day for the service. People came from across Wichita as well as some outlying cities. Quite a celebration and quite a day. At last Chuck was the full-time pastor of a church.

The next Sunday, Chuck held his breath as he stepped into the sanctuary to see how many people had shown up. Well, it wasn't 250. It was seventeen, the people from First Church of God who had said they would go with Chuck if he planted a new church. Behind and in front of them were rows of empty seats. That first Sunday morning was strange and very overwhelming. There Chuck was with a wonderful building, a huge debt, and only enough people to fill three pews. A major problem, a challenge, but instead of ducking it, he hit it head on and with the guidance of the Lord. He set to work to build a congregation.

It took considerable work to fill those pews. Chuck would be the first to tell you that he didn't know how to start a church. No books were available to instruct him. No courses in seminary. He said he wore out his knees and his knuckles—his knees in prayer and his knuckles knocking on doors. And it worked. He made some mistakes, but the Lord honored him anyway. The church grew steadily as a result of Chuck's "knees and knuckles" ministry.

Most of the people who came to Pawnee Church of God lived in the vicinity of the church. There was one older couple, however, who lived on the north side of Wichita and was coming every Sunday. Chuck was curious about why this couple was coming so far, so he decided to ask.

"My brother," Chuck said to the husband one Sunday, "I am most pleased that you come here to church. We love to have you here. But I have a question. You live on the north side of Wichita, and there are numerous churches up there. Why do you choose to drive all the way down here every week?"

"Well, Brother Thomas," the man replied, "it's like this. My wife and I calculated the miles and where else we drive. We really only drive to the grocery, and it's just down the street from us. We decided we'd come here because it is just far enough away that a weekly trip would keep our car's battery working."

It was not the answer Chuck expected, but it was fine. He enjoyed having them even if their reason for coming was unusual.

Beginning a Family

Five months after the opening of the church, on February 17, 1953, Chuck welcomed his first son, Charles Mark Thomas, into the world. Our first son was named Charles after his father and also after my dad, my brother, and Chuck's grandfather Conyers. His middle name, Mark, was from the Bible. We chose to call him Mark at this time; however, he would use the name Charles as he got older. A couple of years later, when Dean Russell Olt of Anderson College was in our home as an evangelist, he told us to look up Psalm 37:37, which says, "Mark the perfect man, and behold the upright" (KJV).

The next family blessing was Paul Stanley Thomas, who arrived May 7, 1957. Chuck was at a conference in eastern Kansas when Paul chose to make his entrance. Having gone there with a friend, Chuck didn't have a car. That challenge didn't stop him from getting back to Wichita for Paul's arrival. He walked and hitchhiked to get home. The arrival of another child was too precious to miss. The name Paul was chosen because of the apostle Paul, a chosen messenger of God. The name Stanley was my maiden name and also that of a well-known Christian leader, E. Stanley Jones.

The third family blessing was John David Thomas, born April 24, 1959. Chuck wanted the name John because of the disciple of Christ whom Jesus loved. He said that name would give his son a special blessing, and adding David, a man after God's own heart, would fit this son even more for his life ahead. With three sons, Chuck felt he had arrived. He felt that he had the ideal family and the ideal pastorate. God was giving him great blessings.

Meeting the Needs of a Growing Church

While Chuck and I were building our family, he was working diligently to build the church congregation. He knocked on every door in all surrounding areas, inviting families to enjoy the services the church provided. He developed a prayer team for direction in staying in the center of the Lord's will. By 1954, the church had grown to the extent it needed a larger gathering space. How could Chuck meet that need with the debt of the current church building? One day he spotted a Quonset hut in a new housing development and asked what was going to happen to it. After being told it was to be sold and moved away, he contacted Vaden Thomson, his friend and a contractor, and asked, "If the building was donated to our church, would you move it for us?"

Vaden looked the building over and answered Chuck. "Yes, if the building were to be donated, it would be worth moving." Vaden was certain it would not be donated.

Another challenge. Due to the zeal of Chuck, the building was donated, and Vaden moved it to the church property in 1955. It added urgently needed space for gatherings, dinners, and even baptisms.

Chuck's commitment to build Pawnee Avenue Church of God and bring people into the kingdom of God was so strong on his heart that he did everything he knew to do to see that the church grew. In the beginning he did everything from leading the singing to cleaning the toilets. By 1957, it was time to add an associate. He contacted Anderson College and met Dale Bengtson. Dale was a music major and ready to graduate. He told Chuck up front that he could stay only two years and then would be going back to Anderson. Chuck offered him the position anyway.

Right after Dale's graduation and his marriage to Linda, the newlyweds headed west to Wichita. Dale became the music director and also worked with the youth. He and Chuck set some ambitious goals and developed choirs for adults, youth, and children, as well as numerous youth activities. Here are some of Dale's recollections of that time.

The church had talented singers with natural voices and keyboard musicians who played piano and organ at a high level. Solo singing and several ensembles were already in place. Chuck played a good trombone and his wife, Donna, was an excellent pianist. When our two years were finished, Linda and I graduated together on the same night at Wichita State University, I with a master of music degree and Linda with a bachelor of arts degree in education. Word got around at the Pawnee Church that we were leaving, and the people presented us with a "This Is Your Life" farewell tribute and generous gifts to support our leap of faith into the next phase of our lives. The TV program "This Is Your Life" was all the rage then, as it chose to honor notable leaders in our country by having the different people they had influenced in their life express their appreciation.

Before he left, Dale enlisted Virginia, an accomplished pianist, to continue the children's choir. She and her husband, Caroldean Briscoe, had responded to one of Chuck's knocks on their door inviting them to this new church, which was in their neighborhood. Virginia was excellent at knocking on doors herself, continuing to enlist kids for the choir and getting it up to around fifty from around the neighborhoods. The children's choir added a great deal to the services for many years. It was very instrumental in bringing the children's moms and dads to church. Many families started coming to see this children's choir. Caroldean served in many capacities in the church and was later featured in the book called *The Greatest Generation*, stories about heroes in WWII, by Tom Brokaw.

From that time on, Chuck always had associates. He took them under his wing, mentoring them to be the pastors and leaders that they wanted to be and building his team. He was also mentoring some of his young people in their leadership development for Christian service. Several went on to become full-time Christian leaders. Dale Bengtson became the Dean of the School of Music at Anderson University. John Lymer, Charlie Briscoe, Keith Rider, Tim Mosteller, Terry Thole, Rodney Thole, and several others went into the pastorate. Darlene Detwiler and Cathy Rider served as missionaries.

A Pastor to God's People

Not only did Pawnee grow in the number of people attending, but it also became a church where people's lives were transformed. Chuck's calling as a pastor was obvious to all who met him. Of the many stories of lives transformed during those years under Chuck's ministry, the one that follows best shows what God was doing through Chuck.

A new family moved into our neighborhood. Fresh from a rural area in South Dakota, they were searching for a career change and were living in a small trailer house in a mobile home park. They wanted a church where they could be comfortable. They visited many but had trouble finding one that wasn't too large and was friendly. One of their new friends in the mobile home park invited them to visit Pawnee. They were surprised as to how friendly it was, so they returned several times. Here is Shirley Rider's story in her own words.

Pastor Thomas's messages on having a personal relationship with Jesus Christ were an entirely new thought to me. This was something we had not heard before, though both of us had attended churches all our lives and in following their rituals, we believed we were Christians.

On Palm Sunday, 1956, Pastor Thomas had an altar call for people to kneel, repent, and accept Jesus as Lord and Savior. Since we had been coming and feeling uneasiness in our souls, we went forward and asked the Lord to be the Lord and Savior of our lives. Immediately the "peace that passeth all under-standing" filled my heart and soul. Unless one has experienced such a life-changing experience, one cannot understand how my thoughts and goals changed.

Through the Sunday school, prayer meetings, special Bible classes, altar training, and many social events, Pawnee Church and Pastor Thomas's leadership of it fulfilled the spiritual and social needs of our entire family for many years. Several lifelong friend-ships developed as we all shared, prayed, and cried together.

In 1962, I became critically ill with leukemia and was in the final stages. Through Pastor Thomas's many counseling ses-sions and hospital visits, I developed assurance and faith to be anointed and prayed over for divine healing. While I was a pa-tient at the Mayo Clinic in Rochester, Minnesota, doctors were able to assure me this miracle had happened. Praise the Lord, I have had no reoccurrence of this disease since!

Throughout the years, innumerable happenings and events have occurred where God's protection and guidance have blessed my family members as well as myself. As difficult as it was for my young family to leave South Dakota so long ago, I thank God for leading me to where his people helped me find a truly fuller and deeper walk with him.

Shirley is a devoted Christian, still opening her heart and life to the callings of the Lord. She is always ready and willing to help when op-portunities come her way. Years later, Chuck preached her husband's fu-neral sermon, which was several years after we had moved from Wichita and actually was his last trip out there before his death in 1992.

Developing a Sunday School

The Lord gave Chuck another challenge when a flyer about a Na-tional Sunday School convention caught his eye. It was offering new ways to build a Sunday school, which was just what Chuck was wanting. He felt Pawnee's Sunday school wasn't developing the way it should. He decided we should drive to the convention in Omaha, Nebraska, to see what we could learn. Those 308 miles across Kansas's wheat fields and through Nebraska's corn country to Omaha was more than we expected, but the convention was well worth the trip. Chuck's head was reeling with new ideas. As soon as he returned home, he set to work to develop a team to implement them across the scope of his Sunday school ministry.

Chuck knew that the Lord had given him a challenge to make significant changes in the neighborhood around the church. Every Tuesday night, many of the congregation gathered, took a list of names and addresses, and became personal visitors and ultimately friends to those in the area. People came to Sunday school because of this personal contact of people caring for them. In two years, the Sunday school attendance grew 40 percent. *Moody Magazine*, similar to *Christianity Today* but published by Moody Bible Institute in Chicago, featured Pastor Chuck Thomas and the remarkable growth of his Sunday school in its September 1960 edition.

The Birth of Corinthian Nursery School

The church continued to grow to the point where once again Chuck saw another need—a place for parents to leave their children while they were working. Women were just starting to get into the work force in great numbers, and they needed good, quality child-care options. Chuck came up with the idea of a nursery school, Corinthian Nursery School. He chose the name Corinthian because he felt that it gave the school a New Testament touch. The apostle Paul had taught at the Corinthian church, and Chuck wanted to teach and, in this case, also provide care for one hundred children.

A nursery school of this size was new to the Kansas authorities, causing them major concern. They were sure a hundred children was too many in one place. The most they had ever considered or ever approved was twenty-five.

"Rev. Thomas," a local authority told him, "we can't approve your school for a hundred children. That makes it too big. We use the number twenty-five as the maximum number for a

"Sir," Chuck responded, "let me show you the building. Here is the main floor with three very large classrooms. Upstairs we have even more space and two staircases as well. Here are the restrooms. We will use the Quonset hut with its kitchen for the lunchroom. The playground is quite large. So, do we have enough space for a hundred children?"

"Why yes, you have ample space and facilities," the man responded, "but we just have never had a school with a hundred children, and we don't want you to have that many."

"Well, sir, this is a church, and we want to reach as many children for the Lord as we can," said Chuck. "With the guarantee of our nation's constitution for the freedom of religion, I don't think you can limit us to twenty-five children when the facilities will handle a hundred or more. I am therefore asking you for an endorsement for one hundred children, and I am expecting you to comply with my request."

There were certainly more conversations, but eventually the authorities gave their permission. Corinthian Nursery School was started in 1962. Chuck asked me to be the director, and I "reported" to him in that role for seventeen years. I often jokingly said that Chuck thought up great ideas and then turned them over to me to work them out. Maybe that was why we made a good team.

Just the Beginning

Yes, Chuck Thomas was a man of dreams and visions. His story was unfolding. His desire was to be useful to the Lord, and he was making a difference in that part of Wichita. But little did he dream of all the Lord had ahead for him. Okay Lord, what's the next step?

Chapter Seven
A PASTOR'S HEART

"Chuck, we are simply outgrowing this house. Look, we've had different groups here three nights this week and had to scramble to find a place for them all to sit. And the boys have run out of space with their toys and their school stuff. Next week you have those missionaries coming from Australia. Where are we going to put them?" I was pointing out another challenge to my husband.

"I know, honey. This house was perfect when we moved in, but that was ten years ago and no kids. How about taking off Thursday this week, and we'll go look for another place?" he said.

Just what do you do with three active sons in only a 1,250-square foot house? Besides, Chuck has having numerous group meetings in the 12-by-13-foot living room, cramming twenty some people at a time into that small space. It was 1960. We had been there ten years, and Chuck felt we could move to a place with more space and still manage it financially. He searched and found a bigger house less than a mile east of the church, at 2035 South Chautauqua. We were about to embark on another new adventure. The reason we could afford it was because it was seriously distressed and for sale at less than half its original asking price.

We moved in July and began the first step in all the needed repair work. The new location was much better for our sons. It was on a half-acre lot, providing room for Chuck to build a play house for the boys and a play house for himself, better known as a barn. He loved having a barn, and this one was the first of three he would build.

Chuck acquired an old Studebaker car about this time and dubbed it "Honeybucket" because of its putrid green color and the fact that it was so rusted out. No gas cap, but a rag would somewhat do. Every time he made a right turn in it, gas would spill out of the gas tank. But with gas at 21 cents a gallon, that did not seem like a big deal at the time. The floors were rusted out. No radio. No heat. But it was transportation for a time.

Then he saw an old 1951 Chevy truck for sale, and a truck was just what he wanted. Buying it, he painted "5 T Ranch" on the doors, since there were five of us Thomas's riding in it. The boys would often pile in the back of the truck and off we would go. Those were the days before it was discovered that it wasn't a safe way to transport anyone. Once the 5 T Ranch truck took us to a vacant lot by the church where a young college student from Gulf Coast Bible College was helping Chuck and our son Mark clean up the lot. The student, in his zeal, stuck the wooden end of a broom through the back window, shattering the glass. Chuck wasn't happy, but he was gracious to the student and told him he would get it fixed. The student appreciated Chuck's grace and forgiveness, even though it cost Chuck the hassle of finding a replacement window for a truck that old plus digging up the money to pay for it. We were a family of five living on $90 a week.

Despite all the problems that we had with that twelve-year-old 1951 Chevy truck, from that point forward, Chuck always had a truck. He loved trucks and had one to the day he died. Somehow he always thought he could be of help to more people with a truck, as it could be used in so many ways. Having a truck for our family and our church was an integral part of this pastor's heart.

Putting the Parable of the Talents into Action

One day as Chuck was preparing his next Sunday's sermon, he had an idea. He had been reading Matthew 25 about the parable of the talents and wondering how that concept would work in our world. It wasn't long before he came in the kitchen, where I was preparing our evening meal, to tell me what he was thinking.

"Donna, I've got an idea. I was reading the parable of the talents, where this man going on a journey gave five talents to one servant, two to another, and one to the other one. You know that mission across town that asked for help? I want to try this talent idea to raise funds for it. We can see how our people will step up to the plate. I can give everyone who wants to participate a $20 bill. (In 1961 twenty dollars was equivalent to about two days' salary.) Then each person can invest it and see what can be done with that money. In say four weeks, everyone can bring back the money and share how the money increased. What do you think? Should we try it? Why not?"

That is exactly what Chuck did the next Sunday. He passed out $20 bills to everyone who was ready to accept the challenge. Four weeks later, it was time to bring in the "talents." What wonderful stories his people shared that Sunday morning. Some baked and sold cookies, another put together a flower arrangement to sell, and one put gas in his lawn mower and mowed lawns for a price. There were all kinds of stories that day and some really interesting investments. The people had put into practice what they had read in the Bible, and the income from that one idea of Chuck's turned out to be a big help for the mission.

Those 110 people that Sunday took $2,200 and turned it into $5,740 by making their talents work for the Lord. And they did it with rejoicing.

A Pastor's Heart for People

The Lord had put his assignment of caring for his people in Chuck's heart, and his response to that assignment began to manifest itself in a number of ways during those years. It began with caring for his parishioners, and it expanded ever wider as Chuck matured in his understanding of Christ's calling on his life.

Somehow the Lord led Chuck to get involved with the juvenile court system. One day he called home and said, "Donna, there is a young boy here at Juvenile Court who could get out if he had some place to go. I was thinking we could help him for a while until he gets on his feet. Would it be okay if I bring him home with me?" I had to think and pray about this challenge, wondering how it would affect our three boys. Chuck said he would monitor the young man's actions, and he would end the arrangement immediately if it was not good for him or us.

That phone call began a series of young juvenile boys from the court staying with us. Sometimes it was only a few days, and sometimes it was a couple of weeks. It didn't create any serious problems, but Chuck did have to set down some rules—no smoking, no cussing, and so on. He brought those young men into our home for some time. One in particular was so eager to learn about the Lord and to learn how he could become useful to the Lord too. That young man later went on to college and became a preacher himself.

After a few especially obnoxious fellows, Chuck called it quits. His sons were growing up, they were impressionable, and he needed to focus on them. In the next several years, some of those young men eventually came back to thank Chuck for his compassion for them.

Meeting Others' Needs

Chuck was always thinking about ways to meet the needs of others. Here are just a few examples.

In 1965, a young man named Larry moved to Wichita and started coming to the church. He had muscular dystrophy, and Chuck discovered he had experienced a very difficult life. Walking and even talking were great problems for him, and yet Larry was going door-to-door selling books, brushes, and various things. He didn't have any other source of income, so his meager sales were just barely putting food on his table and a roof over his head.

Chuck saw Larry's situation as another assignment, another challenge. He decided maybe a golf cart could help Larry get around. Getting one was the first step, but there was also the problem of getting permission for Larry to drive it on the streets. Another problem was training Larry how to drive it and to follow the rules of the road. Chuck recruited some of the men at the church to help. It wasn't long before Larry had a golf cart and was learning how to navigate the streets and traffic. It wasn't easy, but it worked. Larry was overjoyed with this new method of getting around, but he was even happier with the love and attention the men at the church gave him.

On October 10, 1970, one of the founding members of Pawnee Church called Chuck at 4 a.m. saying her husband had just had a heart attack. Here is the story in Icle McTaggart's words.

Chuck was at our house in ten minutes. He followed the ambulance to the hospital. Then he called Donna and two of my friends. They came to the hospital along with my wife and two daughters. As I lay there near death, I heard Chuck say, "Let's pray." It seemed to me like they were all praying at the same time. But I heard Chuck above the rest, pleading with God to spare my life. I will always be grateful to Chuck for being there for me when I needed him the most.

Cathy Lavender, another member of the church, shares her thoughts on Chuck's ministry as well.

When I look back over my life, I realize how hugely my values and life direction have been impacted by the influence of Pastor Thomas. My mother accepted Christ in 1957 at Pawnee Avenue Church of God, when I was four years old. Pastor Thomas later also prayed with my father at the altar at a camp meeting out at Camp Fellowship where he made his commitment to the Lord. As a result, I was raised in a loving home in which Christian values were taught and modeled. I can't count how many church services I attended, hearing Pastor Thomas preach. What impressed me as a youth was the conviction with which he lived and taught. And love always permeated his messages.

It seems Pastor Thomas was a part of many of the big moments in my life over more than forty years. He baptized me as a child in 1961, he taught me through his preaching, he performed our marriage ceremony in 1977, and last, he returned to Wichita to preach my father's funeral in 1991. I distinctly recall the questions he answered in my mother's living room the day before the funeral, and the gentle wisdom and comfort he was able to provide through his prayer and sharing with us.

It wasn't the wisdom, compassion, and love that made Charles Thomas a great man, however. It was his willingness to love God with his entire mind, heart, and soul; his heart for the lost; and his commitment to be obedient in using the gifts God had given him. He and Donna thought outside the box and boldly tried new things to get Christ's message to people. I don't think we will know this side of heaven how many lives God has changed as result of their influence. I am so grateful that I was one of those lives.

Kathy Buffington also remembers a lifetime of experiences with Chuck as a pastor.

My dad and mom were one of the original families that came to Pawnee, so my growing up years were there. My sister and I enjoyed the choir and all the other children and later youth experience. Yes, growing up as a child and a youth under Pastor Chuck was wonderful; however, he would not hesitate to stop in the middle of a sermon and say, "You girls are talking and not listening." He never did it in a mean way but only so we would learn. I can still hear his voice telling our youth group to keep God's word in our hearts.

Family camps, Cowboy Church, mission conventions, and Sunday school contests all happened at our church in a very exciting way. Brother Thomas made church fun and exciting whether we were in the church, at camp, at someone's house, traveling together, or wherever we were—singing, sharing, and always having a good time and learning lessons that would stick with us forever.

When a small group of us wanted to go to the Biannual Church of God International Youth Convention but had no way to get to Boston, Pastor Thomas called a friend, and a pilot flew us in a private plane. As I remember it, other pastors just didn't do those things. Other pastors didn't play with the kids, get dirty, or do repair work on the church (in his overalls). But my pastor did. My pastor gave me a heart for missions and took me there to see it and told me I could help people. These lessons are still in my heart.

Chuck was always looking out for the young people in the church. He met with them every Tuesday night in a venture he called "Quest." Yes, it was an adventure for them to search the Scriptures, to share their problems with friends and at school, and to know that he cared for them and loved them. "What impressed me as a youth was the conviction with which he lived and taught. And love always permeated his messages.

Sunday Nights

Church on Sunday night was a weekly activity in those days. There was good attendance and a warm, friendly feeling. Chuck would lead the singing, sometimes playing his trombone too. Lois Wethington remembers, "I would try to hide behind someone when he would start singing 'Oh How I Love Jesus' because it seemed he would always pick me to do the alternative way of singing that song, which was, 'Oh, Lois, do you love Jesus?' 'Oh, yes, I love Jesus,' I would have to sing, and so on. I suppose he would choose me because I was serving as his office secretary, a position I felt honored to serve in, as I enjoyed working with him."

Chuck started a Sunday night program for the youth he called "Destination Unknown." It was an activity after the Sunday evening service, and it enticed the youth because it was always a surprise. They never knew where they were going or the agenda, as they changed regularly. As other churches heard about this program, their leaders started it for their youth groups.

Terrace Gardens Nursing Homes

Chuck became increasingly more concerned about the elderly and the care he saw them receiving. Among the original seventeen people at the church was an older couple. The husband passed away first, and then his wife began struggling with health. She was placed in a "Ma and Pa Home," which was what passed for a nursing home at that time. Those ordinary houses were used to care for four or five older people that needed nursing care or assisted living. No medical staff was involved.

Some homes were there because of compassion and others as a source of revenue. This older woman in our church became worse after moving into one of those places. Whenever she had to be sent to the hospital, however, she would immediately get better. What concerned Chuck was that there wasn't a good place for her to live when she was doing better and was released from the hospital. Another challenge.

Chuck determined to get some of his doctor friends together and start a good nursing home. It was a new concept, and those were the days before Medicare and Medicaid were available. He enlisted nine doctors (including three Kardatzke family members), and using his drive and energy, they started Terrace Gardens Nursing Home, a 100-bed facility. It was such a huge success that they built another one in Haysville and then one in Olathe and then one in Manhattan, Kansas. When people in other areas heard about these homes, they asked Chuck and his team of doctors for help. They built one in Oklahoma City, Oklahoma; Anderson, Indiana; and in several other cities and states. The homes were expanded in time to have assisted living and retirement apartments. It wasn't too long before Medicare and Medicaid came into being and those nursing homes fit right into the government plan of caring for the elderly.

God works in mysterious ways. Little did Chuck imagine that soon his own family would benefit from his hard work starting nursing homes. When Chuck's dad developed Alzheimer's, Chuck brought him to Wichita for care. Much later, my mom and dad needed care for a short time, so Chuck brought them to Wichita from Florida. My mom soon died in Terrace Gardens in Wichita, and later, when my dad couldn't drive anymore, he moved into one of the apartments.

Chuck had addressed the problem of the lady in his church as to why there was no good place to provide care for her. Once again he turned his "why should he do anything about it?" into his "why not?" challenge. Those nursing homes were on the cutting edge of what is available today and were certainly ahead of the times in the 1960s. They were all started by Chuck Thomas accepting the Lord's challenge and challenging his doctor friends to help.

Cowboy Church

Living in Kansas, Chuck was greatly influenced by the western culture and the numerous cowboys. Although no actual cowboys were coming to the church at the time, Chuck decided to turn one of our Sunday night services into "Cowboy Church." He pulled a team together for this new idea. Men brought in bales of straw, saddles, and horse blankets. Putting them around the Quonset hut gave the right atmosphere. The music director chose western songs and used guitars to enhance the singing. Everyone was encouraged to wear blue jeans and western shirts plus cowboy hats to the service.

There was a great atmosphere of enjoyment in worshiping the Lord in this new way. Following the service there was a huge campfire and hot dogs for everybody. Cowboy Church was a hit. Immediately it became an annual event and jumped to the top of the chart of the unusual and enjoyable events each year.

Christian Woodstock 1969

It was the end of a decade of trouble when Woodstock hit the news. Over four hundred thousand young people called "hippies" gathered in New England to express themselves in every way possible. It was far from anything Christian, but it was in our face on the TV and in the newspapers. In response, Chuck came up with the idea of having a Christian Woodstock out at the church campground, Camp Fellowship. It started on Friday night with bands from various churches and food, of course. On Saturday were more bands, more music, and also some Christian messages that would relate to the youth of that day. Approximately four hundred youth from across Wichita went there and discovered that the hippie concept of a gathering could be used to bring them closer to the Lord.

No, it didn't make the newspaper or TV, but it served the purpose of helping those hippie-aged youth in the area have a "hip" event of Christian celebration and praising the Lord together.

Soldiers in the Church

In 1962, it was discovered that Russia was supplying Cuba with intermediate-range nuclear missiles just ninety miles off the coast of Florida. It seemed that Nikita Khrushchev was bringing the whole world to the brink of nuclear war. President John F. Kennedy readied to send troops into Cuba to protect our country against the threat of the Cold War being right in our backyard. The whole country was on edge. The Cuban Missile Crisis dominated the television, radio, and newspapers for weeks. News was leaking out of Russia and Eastern Europe about Christians being tortured for their faith in God, Bibles being confiscated and burned, and churches being closed and used for cowsheds. Yes, WWII was over, but we were in the midst of the Cold War.

Kansas had missile silos around the state ready to counter a missile from Cuba, which people in our country were told could come at any time. Chuck made plans for our family as to what we would do if a missile were to strike and where we would go to find each other after a disaster. It was a scary time.

Shortly after Castro backed down and sent the missiles back to Russia and things calmed down, Chuck felt he had to deal with some difficult questions. To what extent would he stand up for Christ, no matter what? No matter if soldiers told him to give them his Bible. No matter if they demanded him to close the church. And no matter if they ordered him to renounce Jesus Christ or die. Great questions for him and for everyone else.

Chuck talked with the church elders about those questions, and they decided to bring the questions to the congregation. They planned an "encounter" on a Sunday night. Three of the church leaders dressed in military uniform entered the sanctuary in the middle of the evening church service with their guns in hand and demanded the people in the congregation renounce Christ or line up in front before a firing squad. (We just might have trouble doing this in our churches today, but it was okay then.)

Yes, people recognized the soldiers as part of the congregation, and yes, they knew the encounter was staged, and yet the message was still tremendously shocking. Each one had to make a decision as to his or her allegiance to Christ, even if it meant dying. The first to step forward to the firing squad was one of the older saints. He marched determinedly to the front. Seeing him go forward made it easier for the rest. We all knew it wasn't actually real, but it did make us stop and think. And yes, the whole congregation made the purposeful decision to follow Christ and be his disciples "no matter what" the consequences were.

Camping Ministry

Thursday was Chuck's day off, so our family would often go out to Camp Fellowship after school for family fun time. Camping was our favorite activity. A special treat was our annual family summer trip to Colorado. We all loved the Lake City area. Chuck loved fly-fishing.

The boys and I liked the trails and just the joy of being in the remote areas.

While we were crossing Colorado's Independence Pass one summer, one of our tires had a blowout. Chuck managed to drive on into Glenwood Springs, where he found a tire shop. He and the boys went in to buy a new tire. Another customer in the store came over to Chuck and started a conversation.

"Say, those are great looking boys. Are you having a good time fishing with them?"

"Sure enough," Chuck responded to this stranger. "We've been fishing on Clear Creek in the Collegiate Peaks area."

"Hey fellows, what are your names?" the man asked.

Our oldest replied, "I'm Mark, and my brothers are Paul and John."

The stranger introduced himself as Harry. "Reverend," he said, immediately deciding that Chuck must be a minister if his boys were named Mark, Paul, and John, "it's getting dark soon. I see you've had tire trouble. Do you have a place to camp tonight?"

"No, not really," replied Chuck. "I thought we'd go on west to find a campground."

"Come on over to my place. I've got a big backyard, and you can set up your camp there. We'd be glad to have you."

This new friend, Harry Fischer, then invited our family to join his "tote-gote club" weekend camping trip. Sounded good to us. Tote-gotes were two-wheel mountain bikes that would go anywhere, straight up a hill or straight down. Chuck accepted the invitation, we went biking with them that weekend, and we got the "tote-gote bug," eventually buying two of them. Mark could handle one with Paul on the seat behind him, and Chuck could take John and me on the other one.

Each evening of that camping trip, we all would gather around the campfire and roast marshmallows. About then Chuck would start singing and lead everyone in campfire songs. Then he would give a simple, short message and close with prayer. The people loved it. They asked Chuck to do the same thing every night.

That is the way our "other" congregation started. Well, it wasn't really a congregation, but these new friends wanted us in Colorado with them as much as possible. We were with them many summers. They loved to sing our songs with us, and they always asked Chuck to share "something out of the Bible" with them. Chuck even preached a funeral for one of the men several years later.

Family Camp

Since camping was fun for his family, Chuck thought it would be great for the families in the church to camp too. Camp Fellowship was perfect for this new idea. Chuck chose a place across the lake that was a bit more remote and set the date and time for any families that wanted to come for the first campout. Did they want to go? Yes, they did.

Chuck had our family there at the camp a bit early that Friday night to watch as people rolled in, family after family. Some had small children, some teenagers, and some older adults, but all were there to enjoy the experience, to build a campfire, to roast hot dogs and marshmallows, and to sing together before Chuck brought a message from the Scriptures. Lois Wethington remembers, "We learned to sing 'John Jacob Jingleheimer Schmidt' when Pastor would lead us in choruses around the campfire. We were usually swatting mosquitoes to the beat of the music, but oh, what fun. And then the initiation of the new campers with 'O wha ta goo siam'."

Saturday was a full day too with games, fishing, cooking, and enjoying the time together. Family camp immediately became a tradition. The whole church looked forward to it every summer.

God's Next Plans

Chuck was enjoying raising a family, and at the same time he was enjoying building a congregation. He knew he was called for these purposes, which is undoubtedly why he was always thinking up new things to do and new ways to do old things. He would often ask me, "Honey, what do you think the Lord wants us to do next?" Good question.

Chapter Eight
THIS WORLD IS DIFFERENT

It was1962, and Pawnee Avenue Church was about to mark its tenth anniversary. Chuck decided to invite an evangelist, Rev. Larry DeShay, to come and preach for a couple of weeks. Rev. DeShay had served as a missionary in Guatemala and Mexico. Each evening at our dinner table, he taught our boys Spanish words and phrases.

"Brother DeShay, how do you say 'thank you'?" Paul asked one evening.

"Just say, 'gracias,' Pablo, and you can say, 'por favor' for please. Let me hear you try those words," said Rev. DeShay.

Of course, Marcos (Mark) and Juan (John) got into the conversation too. They started with the words for butter, bread, salt, milk and other things on the table. It turned into a game, as the boys were eager to learn these new words, continually asking the Spanish words for everything from "I don't want that" to "Can I have some more?" and "Is there dessert today?"

As Rev. DeShay became acquainted with our family and the congregation, he noticed our lack of involvement in missions. On his final day with us, he decided to challenge Chuck.

"Young man," he said, "you're not really going to accomplish all the Lord has for you until you get a heart for missions. I think you should take a trip to Mexico and see what the Lord is doing there."

Those words rang in Chuck's heart, and he couldn't forget them. And could he ignore this challenge? Not Chuck Thomas. Once again, he would simply answer the challenge with a "why not?" That December, right after Christmas, we loaded our three boys in the back of our station wagon and started the first 1,000-mile journey of what would become a totally new adventure. God was leading us into his plans for our future. We were experiencing the words in Jeremiah 29:11, "'For I know the plans I have for you,' declares the LORD, 'plans to prosper you and not to harm you, plans to give you hope and a future.'" And what a future!

Crossing the Rio Grande

You could certainly say we were uncomfortable as we crossed the border at Laredo, Texas, and drove across the Rio Grande into Mexico, but it was more than that. We were scared. This was a different country, a different language, different people. We were strangers in a strange land. It was 1962, and Americans didn't go into Mexico. Travel to other countries was not something that the average U.S. citizen did at that time. Yet there we were, the average American family, traveling in a foreign country ourselves to see what missionaries do and why they are needed. Rev. DeShay had told us about Raymond Hastings and his wife, missionaries at La Buena Tierra, the Christian Bible Training School in Saltillo. We were headed there.

Chuck was doing okay as we arrived in Monterrey, although buying gasoline by the liter was totally different and the peso was strange money. He had to do a little arithmetic to figure it all out. Heading on farther west, up the mountains some fifty miles on to the town of Saltillo, the car started acting up. It seemed to be the fuel pump. Chuck didn't see anywhere to get help. He didn't know how to respond in Spanish even if help were offered. There we were in a foreign country with a car in trouble, and we didn't know a soul to ask for help. Those were certainly the days before cell phones too, and our Spanish was limited to basically "por favor" and "si." Considering the options, Chuck chose to try to drive on to Saltillo in spite of the condition of the car. We were praying all the way. The Lord did get us there safely, and the American missionaries, Ray and Ella Mae, were a most welcome sight.

This trip was the beginning of a major change in Chuck and me. The Lord was working on us. We were changing inside as we met, fellowshiped, and worshiped with Mexican Christians. Going to services in the village churches, as well as the church in Saltillo, was a new and different experience. We worshiped together with the people in a language we didn't understand. It was so different from our church in Kansas, but we discovered God was alive and well on the south side of the Rio Grande as well as the north. This experience made Chuck excited to get home and tell his congregation all about it.

Arriving home, Chuck discovered he had a major problem. He had taught his people that missions were not important. The people were not interested. May I repeat? They were not interested. One elder even challenged Chuck by saying, "Missions, who cares about missions." Was the Lord going to let Chuck rest now and forget Mexico? No. This response just increased Chuck's determination to help his congregation see missions in a new way and grasp the full meaning of the Great Commission. Another challenge for Chuck, and he decided to tackle it head on. The problem was, how could he change their concept of missions? What would it take to make them understand?

One day someone in the church asked Chuck, "What's it really like on the mission field?" That was when Chuck turned to me and said, "Let's just take them there and show them." If a trip to Mexico changed us, he was thinking, then maybe that is what it would take to change them. Yes, he would find a way. In the meantime, he had another, more immediate problem.

Race Riots

The hot August heat of that summer provoked the disenfranchised black youth in Los Angeles to demand equal opportunities. Tracking the Watts race riots in Los Angeles, we saw riots were spreading across the US. In those six days of the Watts riots, the contagious effect caught on in Detroit, Chicago, and in several other cities, including Wichita.

Chuck contacted Rev. Wilfred Jordon, his friend and former pastor of the black Church of God in Wichita, to come share with our congregation as to this situation. Rev. Jordon met with Chuck and some of his key people to discuss the opportunities for Christians to respond. Finding out that there was a small ministry in a house on North Estelle, located in the heart of the black community, Chuck inquired how we could help. He was told it would take more than help—that the leader was moving to San Diego and without a new staff, the church would be finished. Hearing about this, a young couple at the Pawnee Church, Loren and LeMoine Ralston and their three children, Jim, Tim, and Joni, stepped forward to fill the gap. They recruited teams from Pawnee to provide Sunday school, Boys and Girls Clubs, mission trips, counseling, block parties, Bible studies, and all kinds of activities.

As this ministry developed, Loren, LeMoine, and Chuck became acquainted with World Impact and brought its assistance into further development of this North Estelle outreach. It was at this point the Lord showed Chuck that missions are reaching people in your own backyard as well as across the Rio Grande. Missions is learning to see the world around you through the eyes of Jesus Christ and to share the compassion for people that he has put in our hearts. More Pawnee people chose to become involved in the North Estelle ministry. And today, over forty years later, this ministry is now stronger than ever and has grown expansively.

Taking Teams into Mexico

With his heart still intent on his people experiencing Mexico, Chuck located a Continental Trailway bus, equal to a Greyhound bus today, that had just come out of service. This 40-passenger bus was in great shape and just what he wanted. It looked like the bus a person would ride from any city to another. The price of the bus was $3,500. That was a lot of money when Chuck's yearly salary was just $4,680. Did he let that challenge stop him? No. He had previously confided in his friend Pete, who had traveled with us to Portland to the International Youth Convention there in 1964, about his desire to buy a bus for mission trips. Unbeknownst to Chuck, Pete had ample resources and offered to help him with a loan. Pete's faith in Chuck enabled him to buy the bus.

Okay, he had the bus. What's next? Since he didn't speak Spanish, Chuck knew he needed an interpreter to start this new venture of taking people into Mexico. He headed to Gulf Coast Bible College in Houston (since 1985, it is Mid-America Christian University and is now located in Oklahoma City). There he met Enrique Cepeda, a new student fresh from Monterrey, Mexico. Enrique readily agreed to be the interpreter. Chuck brought him home and introduced him to the team.

Enrique was a valuable asset to this first trip. He knew the language, of course, but he also knew the culture, which was quite foreign to Chuck. Mexicans also used a lot of gestures that were unfamiliar as well. One was rubbing an elbow as a sign someone was stingy. Enrique helped Chuck and the first team cross the border in Laredo in 1964 and deal with the Mexican border patrol. Of those first forty people on the bus, most were from our congregation. They saw it as a party; they loved Chuck's spirit of adventure, and they were ready to go.

At that time the border patrols were used to bribes. This approach was not part of Chuck's way of life, but Enrique was there to help him deal with them. There were also the problems of knowing where to eat, where to buy fuel, and where the team would stay each night. Enrique solved all those problems, enabling the two-week journey to be enjoyable all the way from Wichita to San Antonio, Monterrey, Saltillo, San Luis Potosi, and on to Mexico City some 1,500 miles.

The first overnight stop was in San Antonio. Chuck had made arrangements there to meet with the Hispanic church so our team would get to know them. That was a good idea. From there we headed on to the border. At the border, we had to watch the patrol go through all our things because we weren't paying the bribe. We made it on to Monterrey, and to our surprise Enrique's parents had dinner ready for us. Enrique gave us a great tour of Monterrey the next day, which climaxed at the church with a special service for us. Enrique was kept busy interpreting for all of us who were trying to have some kind of conversation in a mix of broken Spanish and English with our new friends.

Our next stop was Saltillo at La Buena Tierra Bible Training School. The students were out to welcome us, and we had several sessions with them. Our team was catching the joy of knowing Christian brothers and sisters in another country. It was something they had never even thought of.

Chuck and Enrique

After a couple of days there, visiting village churches, checking out the market, and enjoying the food, we moved on south to San Luis Potosi and then to Mexico City. This experience was all so different from our sheltered life at home. What an adventure. Everyone was enjoying it—that is, all but one. She had brought her own food along because she was afraid of eating the local food. She did change after about a week when she realized no one was getting sick and how much the rest of us were enjoying it.

The first team came back excited about all they had experienced. Chuck planned another trip for the next year and then another. The people on each trip came home as excited as Chuck was. Our three boys got a taste of Mexico on these trips as well.

As word of the trips spread, people from other churches and states were asking if they could go too. Chuck was creating a whole new method of learning about missions. Visiting the mission field in this way was unheard of at the time. Chuck was onto something that really was new and inventive in the "mission world." The idea of short-term mission trips was being discovered, and we were about to change the way people from the United States and around the world thought about missions. Obviously the Lord had his plans, and Chuck was a part of them.

Enrique was a guide several more times. If he couldn't go, he would get one of his sisters or brothers to go with us. The relationship grew to the point that Enrique considered Chuck his other father. Chuck played an important role in Enrique's life too, encouraging him ultimately to earn a degree from Gulf Coast Bible College, a B.A. from Warner Pacific College, his Master of Divinity from Asbury Seminary, and his doctoral degree from Fuller in 1976. Chuck was also Enrique's counsel for his marriage to Lydia and his endorser for his ordination by the Mexican Church of God pastors in Ensenada, both scheduled in the summer of 1969. Here are Enrique's own words about his relationship with Chuck.

> Chuck was there with me when I graduated from Fuller Theological Seminary in Pasadena, California, with my doctoral degree in 1976. An impressive quality of Chuck was his availability. He would put aside his schedule and priorities to serve others.
>
> I also remember riding numerous times with Chuck in his pickup truck, and the many lessons that I learned from him in those short trips. It was in one of those rides that he told me about his vision for Project Partner and his dream about medical evangelism that continues even now, years after he has gone to be with the Lord. How blessed I have been to have him for my mentor, my special friend.

Now with missions in his mind and heart, Chuck chose to start an annual missionary conference at the church. The first was in February 1966. He brought Rev. Forrest Richey, a pastor in Ponca City, OK, who had been developing this type of mission program, to challenge our congregation with the theme, "Are You Hiding the Gospel?" His goal for that event was to raise funds to support Paul and Nova Hutchins and their family in Bangladesh and Darlene Detwiler as a nurse in Kenya. This conference was only two years after the first bus trip to Mexico, but by this time a great many of the congregation had a heart for missions. They were changed. The elder who had said, "Missions, who cares about missions," had radically changed his tune and was one of the supporters. That week, when the congregation was asked to make a pledge for missions, the people pledged over and beyond the necessary funds needed. Their hearts had changed. Missions were no longer just a concept but an integral and vital part of the life of the congregation.

Darlene Detwiler was a young, single woman in the church who had chosen to serve at Mwihila Mission Hospital in Kenya, East Africa. Chuck made a big deal of sending her off with the entire congregation involved. The bus was called into duty along with numerous cars for a procession to the airport. That eventful day caused another young lady in the congregation to resolve that some day she too would go to work there. Many years later, that young woman, Cathy Lavender, along with her husband Paul and their two young children, did just that, serving in Kenya at the same hospital.

Our initial trip to Mexico, terrifying at first and heart-changing throughout, was the beginning of a life journey that would eventually take Chuck and me around the world, not once but many times. Jeremiah 29:11 was meant for us. Chuck's purpose was to do the will of his heavenly Father. He was committed to that. But little did he know the plans the Lord had ahead for him. He couldn't even dream of the fantastic adventures God had waiting ahead.

Central and South America

It was 1966 when a Nazarene pastor challenged Chuck to expand his missions vision and see what the Lord was doing in South America. My mom and dad agreed to come to Wichita and stay with our boys. Chuck made inquiries as to where mission stations were and who the missionaries might be. He discovered that the Church of God only had one missionary in all of the area, and he was in Panama. So we would start in Panama.

Chuck also had heard of a German pastor in Nebraska who knew something about a German Church of God in Argentina, so we drove to Nebraska to see if we could locate him. We did, and the pastor was excited when Chuck told him that we would be going to Argentina to look up the church there. He gave Chuck the name of Andre Bokrand, who lived outside of Buenos Aires, and explained that many Germans had moved to South America after the war to start a new way of life. He also introduced us to a friend who was visiting him but lived in Rondon, Brazil. She offered to meet us at Iguaçu Falls and take us to visit the

German Church of God in Rondon. Chuck had also heard about Paul Butz in Pucallpa, Peru. He had no idea where Rondon, Iguacu Falls, or Pucallpa, Peru were. It wasn't easy to find a map of South America in 1966 either. Chuck did find one and located Pucallpa, way east of Lima in the upper Amazon, so he scheduled a stop to visit Paul Butz too. Iguacu Falls was in Brazil on the Parana River, separating Argentina and Brazil. Rondon was harder to find, as it was just a small town lost in the vastness of Brazil many miles northeast of Iguacu. The rest of Chuck's contacts for the trip were Nazarene missionaries who were all rich blessings and had beautiful hearts for the people they served.

Panama and the San Blas Islands

Each country and each contact with the missionaries and the local church on this journey was a joy and an adventure. Starting in Panama, Dean and Nina Flora met us at the airport and made us more than welcome. They took us on both sides of the isthmus, from Panama City on the Pacific side to Colon, located thirty miles east on the Caribbean. This Pan-American highway connecting both sides of the isthmus was built by the U.S. when the Panama Canal was built in 1899. Chuck and his team were beginning to see a bit of Latin American culture and realizing it wasn't at all like Mexico. There were many immigrants from Europe but also native tribal people. To be sure, the team was gaining an understanding of the hearts of the people. Seeing the beautiful children, eating the unique and delicious food, and just learning about the culture was intriguing and important in the development of Chuck's expanding vision. Already the Lord was working in his heart and mine with the joy of seeing people through the eyes of Christ.

"Chuck," Dean Flora asked on the second day of our visit there with him, "have you ever heard of the San Blas Islands?" Of course he hadn't. Very little about South America was taught in our schools and colleges. Dean continued, "There are 365 islands just off the coast of Panama in the Caribbean, home to the Cuna Indians. I'd like for you to see them. Want to go?"

At that time few foreigners had ever been to the San Blas Islands, and no foreigner had ever been allowed to stay overnight. Dean made arrangements for Chuck and me to fly over in a small Cessna 180 airplane. He wanted us to see what God was doing with these people previously unreached in their knowledge of Jesus Christ. That half-hour flight gave us a wonderful panoramic view of Panama, including its vast jungles, mountains, and lakes. We could actually see both the Atlantic and Pacific Oceans at the same time. Our plane landed on a small strip on the island of Nalunaga (Red Snapper). There really wasn't too much to the island that we could see—just palm trees, bamboo huts, and a boat dock. Dean took us over to the biggest hut, which was the meeting place for the island chief and his council. They were inside, expecting us.

When Chuck stepped inside, he was surprised to see that the chief and his council were waiting for us in typical Cuna style: reclining in their hammocks. Each of them had his own special hammock, and all business was conducted from them. There were three hammocks waiting, one for Dean, one for Chuck, and one for me. It made an interesting conference center (no conference table to sit around).

The Cuna people weren't used to having foreign guests, but they wanted to extend a special welcome to us. The chief asked many questions, including where Chuck was from and what he knew about Jesus. The people seemed very eager to learn more about the Lord. Their knowledge of the rest of the world was extremely limited, so this visit seemed a good opportunity for them to learn from Chuck.

Later, walking among the huts, Chuck was a unique sight to the Cunas. The fact that he was more than six feet tall created a lot of laughter and finger pointing among the children. But they were unique to us as well. The women's blouses featured interesting patterns of reverse appliqué depicting important aspects of their culture. They each wore a nose ring and had a black line painted down their nose to make it appear longer, a sign of beauty in their culture (just like shiny painted lips in ours). Their skirts were simply a piece of material tied around the waist. Over their heads they wore red shawls. The little girls all wore panties, and the little boys nothing at all. Their sustenance came from fishing and growing corn on the mainland of Panama. They crossed the water in their handmade dugout canoes to plant and tend to their crops there, since space was so scarce on the islands. Their meals were simple: roasted fish, corn, rice, coffee, and bread. Their system of exchange was mostly by barter.

Dean took us over to a bamboo hut. Going inside, we saw a few boards to sit on, and we soon understood that this was the church. The Cuna Indians had met Jesus. As we worshiped with them there in that bamboo church, we came to see them as our brothers and sisters in the family of God. They certainly didn't look like our congregation at home, but we gained a warm appreciation for them. Chuck was invited to speak, and his purpose was to encourage them in their relationship with the Lord. Fortunately they had the Bible in their language. Chuck's words opened the door for him to build a blessed relationship that gave them joy and a greater understanding of the kingdom of God.

The way the Cunas had met Jesus was unique, but then the Lord usually does things that way. God used a Cuna fisherman called Brother Jimmy. He was a sailor. Early in his life, he had hired on to a big commercial vessel, and in that process he learned English before he returned home to Nalunaga. Then in 1959, a missionary came to Panama: Dean Flora. Dean heard about the San Blas Islands from a seat companion on the Pan-Am plane that brought them to Panama. Within four months, Dean met Jimmy. Shortly afterward Jimmy's little boy, Freddy, became very ill. Jimmy asked Dean to bring a doctor to Nalunaga to examine his son. The next day Dean was there with a Christian doctor who gave the boy some medicine. Freddy was seriously ill, but after Dean and the doctor left, the local medicine man told Jimmy to throw the medicine away. The medicine man had better potions for him, he said. Jimmy obeyed the medicine man. In three days, Freddy was dead.

Jimmy went to Dean and said, "I loved my son, but God knows all this. I want to pray to God." Jimmy prayed. Then, realizing that the medicine man's decision had led to the death of Jimmy's little boy, the Cunas wouldn't let the medicine man back on the island. They were ready to find Christ, the true Healer. Jimmy was the first one to choose to become a Christian. Through the death of his son and the compassion of Dean, Jimmy put his trust in the Lord. Because of him, many of the Cuna Indians came to the Lord, and a strong church was formed across several of the San Blas Islands.

South American Nations

Dean had us go to several churches in Panama before we flew on to Medellin, Colombia, to visit the Oriental Missions Society (OMS) mission station. Our three days there were used to visit churches and learn more about OMS. An unforgettable memory was one morning service at a church when it was pelted with rocks the whole time. To us, it was most strange to have the church pelted with rocks during a service, but the people told us it was normal for our Colombian Christian brothers and sisters. The local people didn't want their religion.

Our third stop was Ecuador and HCJB radio for another three-day visit. What a world was opening up before our eyes. Coming from our culture, we would never expect so many people were living in such different conditions and with such little understanding of Jesus. Each mission station was an oasis and felt like a safe haven, since the presence of Jesus was with us there. Each mission was also unique and so needed as a base camp to spread the gospel. HCJB was making a significant difference too. Having read the book, *Through Gates of Splendor*, by Elizabeth Elliot, Chuck inquired about the legacy of Jim Elliot with the Auca Indians. We were escorted some thirty miles through the jungle to Sands, the base camp of the missionaries to this tribe. It was awesome to hear their stories and feel their commitment to share the gospel.

Lima, Peru, was the next visit with some Nazarene missionaries. They too had awesome stories to tell. Their lives were committed to taking the gospel to the hundreds of thousands of people living in refugee camps around Lima in shacks made of improvised cardboard or strips of tin, no sanitation, few jobs, only barrels for collecting the water that was used for drinking, cooking, and bathing.

From there we took a Peruvian Airways flight over to Pucallpa, located on an Amazon River tributary, to see what missionary Paul Butz was doing with his Bible school. What an interesting night we spent on a bed only three feet wide for the two of us. Throughout the night we could hear creatures, probably rats or mice, in the wall beside our bed. It helped us grasp what everyday life was like in other places and other countries. Chuck liked to say it gave us "a different perspective." But it was great to meet Paul Butz's students and see the impact they were having in that unique part of the world.

La Paz, Bolivia, came next. Its unique beauty and high altitude of 11,811 feet figuratively and literally took our breath away. The missionaries there escorted us outside of town to a large tent for a Christian service. Chuck had the privilege of preaching to the Aymara and Quechua Indians. It took some time, as his message had to be translated three times—from English to Spanish, then to Aymara, and then finally to Quechua. The people were dressed so differently than we had observed anywhere else in South America. The women wore bowler hats and full, colorful skirts, and the mothers wore a shawl on their backs with a baby in it. The men had big loose shirts and plain pants, and their hats were big enough to keep all the sun off their faces. They seemed so receptive to the gospel.

From La Paz we flew on to Santiago, Chile, for only a brief stop to personally explore that city by ourselves, and then we were on another flight over to Buenos Aires, Argentina. In Buenos Aires, Chuck wanted to find that German church the Nebraska pastor had told us about. We discovered we had to take a train some distance to a suburb and then a taxi to locate it. The German people met for church in a storefront building, but fortunately we found the home of the pastor, Andres Bokrand. He and six of his people seemed to be waiting for us, although he didn't know we were coming. The pastor's wife quickly produced a drink for us called Mate, a hot native drink. We discovered later that everyone drinks Mate, and continually. The only trouble was that they only had one cup and one silver straw for all nine of us to use to drink, which is the custom. That cup was passed around, and I was at the end of the line. Chuck whispered for me not to worry. We couldn't offend these new friends by refusing their drink. They were so gracious. These people and many more had left Germany and moved to Argentina after the war to rebuild their lives.

Flying up to Iguaçu, Brazil, we were surprised to land on a grass strip without a terminal building. The biggest surprise was that we were still in Argentina. All the passengers on our flight climbed in the back of a small truck, so we did too. It took us to the Paraná River. Chuck started down the steep bank there, saying, "Come on. We'll see where this takes us." Waiting at the water's edge were some rowboats. If we wanted to go to Brazil, we had to get in a boat. No immigration, no customs—just get in the boat on the Argentine side and get out in Brazil. This approach to travel gave us some concern because we had always had our passports stamped when we entered a country and presented it again with the stamp on it when going through immigration to depart. But we had no choice there.

Our contact in Brazil was to be Tabitha Meier. Her family had also come from Germany. We were to find her in the small town near Iguaçu Falls. The Falls were amazing, much bigger than our Niagara Falls. In 1966 this was not the tourist attraction it is now, and there was little commercial activity. After checking a couple of hotels, we were about to give up finding Tabitha. Then we entered the lobby of the last hotel and there she was waiting for us.

The next morning she took us to the bus station for an all-day ride to Rondon, a village of mostly German immigrants. The people at our destination were having camp meeting, German style. They were delighted to have us and had even planned the dedication of one of their small frame churches while Chuck was there so he could be a part of it. We were definitely in the middle of nowhere. No paved streets anywhere, just the red dirt and lanterns in the church. The beds had straw ticks for mattresses and were only five and a half feet long, which was a problem for Chuck, who was a six-foot-two man. But the people were our brothers and sisters in the Lord. Their German band played for every church service and added a lot of spark to the meetings.

Here we met up with Pastor Ruben Malzon. He had spent twenty-four hours riding on a bus from Curitiba to see us. He asked us to come to his church in Curitiba, so that became our next stop. What a reunion Chuck and Ruben had, reliving their World War II experiences. When they started talking about the war, they quickly discovered they were both in the same battle on the Moselle River. It didn't matter that Chuck was with the American army and Ruben was with the German army. What mattered was that they were brothers in the Lord, and the Lord had brought them both out alive and with purpose in their lives for serving him.

Our final stops were in Sao Paulo and Rio de Janeiro. Those cities were brimming with people, people from many European countries as well as native Brazilians. We met some great Nazarene missionaries who helped us understand the mix of religions in Brazil, Catholicism with superstition, and the practice of voodoo.

On the flight home to Wichita, we wondered how we could process all of the experiences we'd had. What a world we had seen, from Wichita to Panama to Brazil and back. We had been among the Cuna Indians, the Quechua, Ayamara, Cariocas, Amerindian, and Choco tribes, as well as many migrants from Spain, Germany, and across Europe. We were in awe at the majestic Andes; the world's highest lake, Titicaca; the huge statue of Christ of the Andes in Rio; the density of the jungles; the roar of the mighty Amazon; and the diverse cultures, languages, and peoples. Our special joy was meeting with the missionaries and hearing their heart cries as we were learning to see the multitudes through the eyes of Christ. The Lord seemed to be talking to Chuck again, saying, "Okay, Chuck. What are you going to do about all of this?" Another challenge. Chuck was already considering what his next step would be and how the Lord would want him to meet this challenge. His desire, as always, was to be God's servant in every way.

Our sons were waiting for us when we came off the plane in Wichita. We had been gone a little over two weeks, but it seemed like two months. They were so eager to hear about the different countries and experiences and see the items we brought back. What a joy to tell them. Chuck thoroughly enjoyed sharing the stories and giving them a taste of another world, a strange and unknown world to them as it had been to us.

Challenge and Response

These trips were not the end of Chuck's mission journeys. They were only a small flame for the beginning. God's challenge for change would expand to include a life Chuck never dreamed of. After he was home, he discovered he was reliving so many of those South American experiences. It was as though the Lord was nudging him and saying, "There is more than Mexico. What about the rest of my world? You were obedient in getting the bus and taking people to see for themselves. Can you find a way to take people to see Central and South America and experience and feel what you are feeling? Find a way, Chuck Thomas, and give others the worldview that you now have. There is a way, and I will help you as you step out in faith to find it. Why not?"

Chapter Nine
WOW!

"I have now seen a world I never knew existed" was Chuck's reaction to the journey through Central and South America. If he couldn't explain Mexico to the people in the church without taking them there, how could he explain what the Lord had put on his heart in these other countries? He couldn't take the bus to South America, so his mind was busy thinking about how to get people all across Latin America and the Caribbean too. What were the options? How could it be done? These were his questions voiced around the dinner table. Our sons liked those questions, and one of them came up with the idea of an airplane. Certainly a bus wouldn't work. A boat would be too slow. Yes, we needed an airplane. Our sons liked it. An airplane was an exciting idea and a bit crazy too.

Chuck had learned to fly when he was still in college. He started with a single engine Piper Cub, and he moved up to a single engine Cessna 172 when he joined a flying club. That experience was in 1949 and the early 1950s. Flying was one activity he really enjoyed. Maybe this idea was the answer to getting more people to experience missions.

Chuck and our boys started the search for a plane in the early spring of 1969. What plane? A DC-3 maybe? Fortunately we were living in Wichita, which at the time was known as the Air Capitol of the World. Our congregation was quite involved in aviation. Boeing, Beech (now Ratheon), Lear, and Cessna aircraft all had factories across the city, plus the large McConnell Air Force Base was there too. Although planes were not a novelty in 1969, travel by plane was still not done by the masses. And who back then had ever heard of a church having its own airplane? Besides, a plane cost a ton of money, required an aircraft mechanic to keep it ready to fly, and needed a place to park. A crazy idea. But did that stop Chuck? Of course not. Remember he liked challenges, and this was certainly a big one.

Chuck's search eventually led him to a Convair 240, a type of airplane going out of service with Japan Airlines. It could seat forty passengers plus crew members, just what we needed to transport our teams. Convairs were manufactured from 1947 to 1956 and were used first by American Airlines. President John F. Kennedy used one on his campaign trail. This particular plane had been taken out of service and flown back to Love Field in Dallas to be sold. Chuck headed for Dallas to see it. When my phone rang several hours later, it was Chuck.

FLYING THE WESTERN HEMISPHERE FOR THE CHURCH

The Convair 240

"Donna," he said, "I've found the one we need. It is great. We can take as many people as we take on the bus. Forty-passenger, twin engine, lots of room, and it won't take much work to get it back in the air. I'm checking on it now. Pray with me about it. I'll be home tonight and have lots more to tell you."

In all his excitement, Chuck forgot to mention the price. When he returned home, he had with him a picture of the plane and information on its performance. And he also had the price. It was $35,000. Our annual salary at the church then was $5,200. The bus had cost one-tenth of the amount of this plane, and we had thought buying it was a major decision back then, a huge step of faith. What did God have in mind for us next? Chuck was about to find out.

Project Partner with Christ

There was much more involved in his new challenge than just finding a plane and buying it. To use it for its intended purpose, Chuck would have to form a 501(c)(3) nonprofit corporation. And he was going to have to raise funds for this new venture. Yes, money, lots of it. These challenges were all new to him and certainly new for a pastor. No classes in college for adventures like these.

Chuck's attorney friend Justus Fugate offered to help. He was a tremendous blessing. He called us to his office and presented us with corporation papers and bylaws. Then he turned to Chuck and said, "What will you name this corporation?"

Chuck looked at me, and I stared back, a bit bewildered. A name? We hadn't thought of that. Scratching his head, Chuck offered, "How about Project Partner? I know a mission group named Project Concern, and I like that name. Project Partner would probably do. We do want to partner with people and countries, and we will have projects. Is that okay, Donna?" I nodded in agreement. I didn't have a clue what we should name it, and Project Partner sounded all right to me.

We left our friend's office feeling as though we were walking on a cloud. Mr. Fugate was always there to help us and had told Chuck many times that his purpose was to keep him out of trouble. Once again, God had provided what was needed for the next step of Chuck's new adventure.

Buying the Convair 240

Next came the really interesting part—actually buying the plane. Here is how it happened.

Our son Mark was in Mexico that summer of 1969 with our friend and translator for our trips to Mexico, Enrique Cepeda. Mark was staying with Enrique while he was attending the International University in Mexico City to learn Spanish. He was there when Enrique and Lydia were married on August 5. The newlyweds and Mark then headed out on a bus (a 24-hour trip) to Ensenada to meet up with us. Chuck and I headed out with our sons Paul and John in a borrowed Cessna 182. We stopped first in Dallas to look at the Convair. Right there, after checking it out again, on August 5, 1969, Chuck signed the purchase agreement. We then flew on to Ensenada, Mexico, to meet up with Mark, Enrique, and Lydia.

In Ensenada, Chuck participated in the ordination service for Enrique during the ministers meeting there. Enrique still quotes today the advice Chuck gave him. "Enrique, you don't have to be successful, but you must always be faithful." The next day after the ordination, we headed home with our three sons to start the process of getting the plane to Wichita.

To pay for the plane, Chuck knew he had to find donors. Fundraising was new for him. The price of $35,000 plus the cost incurred in getting the plane airworthy and the hours of practice required to get Chuck's pilot licenses upgraded to fly a Convair was a major mountain to climb. He had a deadline too, as he had already committed to a trip in November to visit the churches in Panama. He started raising the funds by contacting our relatives and close friends. They were encouraging and made donations—one as large as $3,000. He was making progress, but still had a long way to go.

At the same time as he was raising the needed funds, he had to spend several weeks in Dallas working on the plane. Everything had to be checked and readied to pass the Federal Aviation Administration (FAA) inspection. Everything! He had to learn each system, and even though he already had his commercial and instrument pilots rating, he had to get this type rating for the Convair. That step meant practicing take-offs and landings and other maneuvers plus the final flight test. He had to hire an instructor there in Dallas as part of the process of getting his type rating.

Everything he was doing cost money we didn't have. Money for the instructor. Money for fuel to fly the plane. And money for repairs. The plane was being prepped by some Delta Airlines mechanics. If they said the plane needed a certain part, Chuck told them to get it. The radios had to be replaced. Okay. New tires? No problem. Additional radios? Go buy them. His purpose was to get the plane in tip-top shape. If he were going to put forty passengers in that plane plus the crew, he certainly didn't want any risks in getting the plane airworthy.

The cost of owning an airplane would include other costs. The plane would have to be flown regularly, at least once a week, to keep everything working and functioning properly. Those trips would cost money too. The fuel costs for those trips were the highest, but there were airport charges as well. Owning a plane and keeping it airworthy cost a ton of money. Knowing this, Chuck chose to make his bed each night on the ground under the Convair instead of incurring the additional cost of a motel room. After all, it was summertime, and he was in Texas.

Chuck was blessed to have many people in our congregation who were involved in aviation. They bought into this adventure with their spirit, offering any help they could. Some even shared some of Chuck's pastoral duties so he would be free to get the plane in the air.

In spite of these challenges, Chuck stepped out in faith to plan the first trip with the plane. He scheduled us to fly from Wichita to Panama in only three months. Since we had taken people on trips with our bus for the past five years, we had developed a small mailing list and somewhat of a reputation. We sent out information on this first airplane trip, and numerous people responded. It wasn't difficult to fill up the plane for that first flight, as what we were doing was unheard of and certainly caught people's attention. Every seat was reserved in a matter of a few weeks after the letter went out. People were coming from Illinois, Missouri, and Oklahoma, as well as Kansas. They were sending in their money and making plans to arrive on Tuesday night, November 19th. Chuck had scheduled the trip to depart on Wednesday morning.

It was not easy to figure out in advance what the cost per passenger for this trip would be. Without knowing how many people we actually would have by departure day, we had to divide the expense of fuel, flight service, pilot expenses, airport fees, and other costs by our best guess. Every trip would be a financial gamble. We also had to cover the maintenance costs, and in aviation that can be quite high. We had to have an A & P licensed mechanic to work on the plane, a commercial type rating to fly it, and trained flight attendants to care for the passengers. And we had to determine in advance where we were going to park the plane and how much that would cost. We set the cost for this trip by faith at $290 per person for all expenses.

With the help of his friends, Chuck had the funds he needed for the purchase of the plane, but just two weeks before the departure day he still had a problem. He was $10,000 short of what was needed to cover all of the expenses. Five thousand of that $10,000 was to cover the costs of the trip, and the other was to pay for the Dallas expenses. Those were nonnegotiable expenses, and the money simply had to be in his hands by the morning of our departure, Wednesday, November 20.

That pressure had Chuck working up proposals and meeting with potential donors. They basically told him they would consider it, but they needed to check with their CPA or their spouse. He was told he could check back with them next week. One week from the November 20 deadline, he was back knocking on their doors, only to find out that they had "gone fishing" or their CPA said it was not a good idea. On Sunday, three days before departure day, we earnestly prayed again for the $10,000 and then tried to forget about it the rest of the day.

Monday morning Chuck went back to the problem. The first call was to a doctor whom he had never met. Chuck talked to his wife, and she said they did plan to make a donation. They talked further, and he was able to ask her how much they planned to contribute. "Would $10,000 help?" she asked. I was sitting at the table beside him and could tell this conversation was special by his expression. Covering his excitement, he managed to ask calmly when he could pick up the check. Her response was for him to pick up the check on Tuesday at 2 p.m. Wow! How the Lord does answer prayer!

Chuck was certainly at the doctor's office at 2 p.m. that Tuesday afternoon, and from there he went immediately to meet me at the bank. He able to cover the Dallas expenses and had the $5,000 in his pocket for the departure the next morning at 5 a.m.

Oh, if you could only ask Chuck if he believed in miracles. God's miracles had cared for him in the foxholes, and this was certainly one with the airplane. Almighty God was his heavenly Father, his Savior, his guide, his provider, and the one Chuck wanted to serve and please with all his heart.

The First Project Partner Eyewitness Crusade

The next morning forty passengers boarded the Convair 240 for the first adventure of Project Partner's Eyewitness Crusades. More than half of them were first-time flyers, so it was an additional new experience for them. The flight left Wichita that morning at 5 a.m. The first stop was in Dallas to pick up the life jackets and rafts that were needed for this over-water flight. The next stop was Galveston to refuel before heading across the Gulf of Mexico. The fueling attendants were expecting the plane, but they weren't expecting a plane as big as the Convair. The reciprocal engines on the Convair used a lot of oil. Refueling didn't take long if the oil was supplied by the gallons, but in Galveston the attendants only had quarts. The fueling process took ninety minutes more than Chuck had planned, giving him concern about the time factor for the rest of the trip.

The first "over-water" segment of the flight went well, as we headed for Merida, Mexico, on the Yucatan Peninsula for more fuel. From there, our route headed toward the Swan Islands, across the Caribbean, and on to San Andres Island for the last fuel stop before arriving in Panama. With the stop for the life jackets and rafts and the fueling delay in Galveston, we were running late. As Chuck radioed our position to the Swan Islands, the controllers informed him there was a storm ahead, but it shouldn't be a bother to us. He headed the plane on south, and because of the earlier delay, it was getting dark.

The storm caused our plane to start bouncing around a bit. Those first-time flyers began to get frightened with the storm's turbulence. Chuck had arranged for me to be trained as a flight attendant, so it was my job to keep everybody comfortable. He called me forward and told me to get on the microphone and tell the people about the $10,000 miracle the day before. He wanted them to know that since God has taken care of us then, he would also take care of us today, through any storm.

Shortly after the passengers heard about God's miracle, we started our descent. As we came out from under those dark clouds, there was the landing strip on San Andres Island—right in front of us. While the plane was being fueled and the passengers were out stretching their legs, Chuck took the opportunity to remind them of the scripture in Hebrews 13:5, "Never will I leave you; never will I forsake you." In spite of the storm and probably because of the miracle story, they all were enjoying this new adventure of an airplane trip and visiting a foreign country.

All of our experiences in Panama went well. The Lord worked on our team members' hearts just as he had on ours on our first trip there. Our times with the Panamanian church and the trip to the San Blas Islands made a great impact on them. They were changed. This new way of taking people to the mission field was working. It was an excellent way to help them get a heart for missions and to realize they too had a responsibility for the Great Commission.

After we returned home, as Chuck was discussing the trip with some of his friends one day, he said, "Seems like faith and money, or the lack of it, often go together. The fact that the Lord supplied the $10,000 is bottom-line evidence that we are doing what God planned for us. This is the kind of confirmation we all need."

Now What?

Wow! That adventure was sure different. Whoever thought of turning an airplane into a mission experience? It was life changing for everyone who'd ventured to climb on board, including Chuck. Can you hear Chuck praying, "Okay, Lord, what is the next step in this adventure?"

We started planning another trip to Mexico City. About that time he heard about a church in Indiana that wanted to take a team to help in Panama. Maybe they would like to go in the Convair. He'd call them and see if they would like a private plane for their trip. He called the Meridian Church in Indianapolis, and were the people there ever surprised at being able to have a plane just for them. It was great for them and great for Project Partner. Just what Chuck wanted. They only wanted the transportation, which meant that all the leadership of the team was in the hands of their mission leader.

Chapter Ten
THE HEART OF A FATHER

Chuck was always thinking about the future of our sons. It was time to take them on a trip to show them what another part of the world was like. The Meridian Church trip was perfect. With his sons' intense interest in the airplane, he knew they would love this adventure. So there we were, all five of us going together on this trip. Another new experience. It would to be great and no responsibility for him after we arrive. In Panama we would have twelve days as a family to explore all the sites—the Panama Canal; the Pacific beaches; the Caribbean beaches; and the rivers, villages, and remote areas of this famous isthmus.

Chuck, Donna, Mark, Paul, and John

Together in Panama

What a great family time and learning experience it was for us. Chuck rented a car and we drove around Panama City, then on the highway across the isthmus and on to the city of Colon on the Caribbean side of the country. While we were in Colon, we stayed in a small hotel in the center of the city. Once in the middle of the night, we were awakened suddenly by our beds sliding across the room. Because a band downstairs was playing so loudly, Chuck thought at first that the noise level had caused the beds to slide. The next morning, we discovered we had experienced a major earthquake. It was amazing that our hotel was not damaged and we were not hurt. The locks on the great Panama Canal that raised and lowered the water level so ships could pass back and forth between the Atlantic and Pacific oceans, however, had considerable damage.

Those days gave us time to explore and enjoy many of the beaches. We had come from the January cold of Kansas to the warmth and sunshine of Panama. That warm ocean water and the hot sun were so different. It was also a great experience to watch the ocean liners being raised and lowered by the canal locks as they changed the water level. We didn't have anything like that in Kansas.

Chuck was carrying a lot of cash given to him to manage by the trip's team leader for return expenses. Chuck always kept all of the money on him, but in this case it wasn't a safe thing to do, so he and the boys put together a strategy. When we were walking down the street, John was always on one side of him and I was on the other. Paul and Mark were right behind. Chuck figured this approach would take care of any would-be pickpockets, and he was fairly certain that no one would dare go after a whole family. It evidently worked, and we never had any trouble at all.

Panama is a melting pot of cultures. In Colon, we enjoyed eating at a Chinese restaurant even though it was strange to be served Chinese food by people speaking Spanish. What we liked best about that place was their sweet and sour pork. Chuck and the boys decided at that moment they wanted me to make sweet and sour pork when we got home. Of course I did, and it is still a family favorite, always reminding us of our adventures in Panama.

Departure Time

The two weeks were over and it was time to go home. Chuck had told the Meridian Church team to meet us at the airport at 8 a.m. sharp or he would go without them. That morning the five of us climbed into our little rented car and headed to the airport, planning to be there early. Unfortunately, Chuck took a wrong turn and we were on the road heading across the isthmus. A police checkpoint was just ahead, and we were supposed to stop. But Chuck had a problem. The accelerator pedal was stuck. Just as we were going past the checkpoint, Chuck took his foot off of the pedal and bent over to release it with his hand. He wanted to know why the boys and I were laughing so hard. We were wondering what the police thought when they saw a car zooming down the road with passengers and apparently no driver. By this time we had discovered we were on the wrong road. Chuck turned the car around and got us to the airport. Everyone was already there, waiting for "this pilot" who had told them to "be sure and be prompt."

Family Times at Camp Fellowship

Chuck enjoyed thinking up new things to do with our sons. Camp Fellowship in Kansas was a very special place for us. It was only twenty miles from our house, and we could steal away and enjoy times out there together as a family. He chose Thursdays right after school for us to go there and spend the night in the Manor House, a two-story house that had been built on the lake by the previous owner. No one else was at camp, so we were free to use the whole place. We either took our supper with us or roasted hot dogs over a campfire.

The boys and Chuck liked to hike around and explore. They also liked to shoot guns. He taught them about guns and how to shoot, first their BB guns and later his 22 rifle and 38 caliber pistol. They would shoot at cans set up on posts to improve their aim. At bedtime, Chuck and the boys would haul in mattresses from another room, spreading them out on the floor in front of the fireplace. We would have popcorn and s'mores and then curl up in our sleeping bags to spend the night. Those Thursday nights were special.

After Labor Day when all scheduled activities at Camp Fellowship were over for the summer, Chuck would take us there to enjoy the swimming pool. It wasn't scheduled to be drained until weeks later, so it was completely ours for a time.

Chuck had joined a group of doctors who enjoyed flying, and together they owned a Cessna. Whenever he could, he loved to fly our family to Camp Fellowship and land the Cessna in the field beside the camp. It was a short, grass runway, and he had to dodge the house at the end, but he made it work and gave us a great time. Chuck actually held a fly-in for some of his Kansas friends out there. Five or six planes—Mooneys, Pipers, or Cessnas—brought them to the camp. That was exciting.

Off to Colorado

Colorado was becoming more a part of Chuck's vacation dreams. We looked forward to planning our family vacations there each year. He would say Colorado was in his blood. We loved going there for our annual camping trips. Our first trip started in the south central part of the state on the Conejos River with a tent. It was there my dad taught Chuck how to fly-fish. As we ventured further west, we discovered the Lake City area. One special attraction was a huge sawdust pile. It must have been thirty or so feet tall, and the boys loved to slide down it. Another attraction was a ghost town, empty and eerie. We camped up Henson Creek about as far back as we could go without a four-wheeler.

Chuck discovered that grasshoppers were some of the best bait for trout. He would take his old brown hat and when he saw some of them, throw his hat on top of them. Then he would reach under the hat and bring those grasshoppers out one by one to put in the Mason jar he had ready. When he had enough grasshoppers in his jar, he'd put on his waders and grab a couple of sandwiches, a candy bar, and one of the boys and head up the creek to fish. He loved to do that.

We traveled and camped all over Colorado, from Durango to Steamboat Springs, from the Collegiate Peaks to Estes Park, and from Sunbeam to Ouray. Our choice location eventually became the Flattops. We loved the remote areas. As soon as we made camp, he got his fishing gear together. The tote-gotes we purchased were winners too. What people call trail bikes today we called tote-gotes back then. They enabled us to see much more of the remote areas back in those beautiful mountains.

Important Lessons

Chuck was very intentional about raising his sons, making sure they learned what they needed to learn when they were young. He saw to it that John and Paul were enrolled in the Young Hunters Safety Clinic. Kansas had just started these clinics, and he wanted to be sure his boys knew how to handle a gun. The thing to do in the fall in Kansas was to travel west and hunt pheasant. It was the sport of choice, and he took the boys many times for that kind of outing, tromping through the fields and hoping to scare up a bird or two.

Chuck taught his boys how to handle a saw, a hammer, and other tools. Mark was given the task of building a little house that was about 10-by-15 feet. We called it the honeymoon cottage. It was out in the middle of the forty acres of farmland we had purchased southeast of Wichita. Some used lumber had been piled there, so Chuck showed Mark how to use it for construction. He enlisted the boys to help him build his first barn behind our house in Wichita, then one on those forty acres close to the honeymoon cottage, and the last one was behind what eventually was our last house together in Ohio.

With all the hay on those forty acres, Chuck decided that his sons needed some farm lessons. He borrowed a baler and taught them the skill of baling hay. It was not necessarily a skill they needed to keep, but it was fun. He also taught them how to use their hands and make things work, whether it was a carburetor, a lawn mower, a truck, a faucet, or an electric fixture. Those lessons were valuable gifts to them.

Most importantly, when opportunities came up, he taught his sons to say "why not?" to challenges and opportunities. This lesson was apparent when he helped Mark as a sophomore at Anderson College. Mark was having some success selling guitars and instruments to his friends and neighbors in the dorm, so it seemed to make sense to start a guitar shop in a storefront in the little nearby town of Chesterfield. Chuck took him to a trade show in Chicago and then taught him how to advertise, handle inventory and equipment, do accounting, manage customers, and just make things work as issues presented themselves. Mark called his business Midwest Music Services. It gave him some income he needed there in college.

More Family Fun

Chuck started a Christmas family tradition he called Daddy's Goodie Table. He started it about the time John was learning to walk. Every Christmas Eve, he put himself in charge of putting all kinds of "goodies" on the coffee table. This was a free-for-all. The family could eat anything they liked and forget about nutrition for that night. He put cheeses, meats, candies, cookies, fruit, pickles, crackers, chips, and anything else he could think of on that table.

Chuck liked tractors and had one in Wichita. When we moved to Ohio, he was able to buy a brand new Ford tractor, and thoroughly enjoyed taking his grandkids with him around the farm. He always had hayrides for the family in the fall along with roasting hot dogs in some remote spot.

Culture Education

Chuck was intentional about helping our sons learn about other cultures. He remembered how little he knew about the world as a child, and he treasured the great experiences he gained in knowing friends in many countries through Project Partner trips. In 1969, he arranged for Mark to go to Mexico City, stay with Enrique Cepeda, and study Spanish at the University of the Americas. We took all the boys to Mexico that summer and on our way home left Mark with Enrique. Enrique was the dean of a Bible college at the time, which made that summer an especially good experience for Mark.

For Paul, it was Guatemala City for his Spanish education. Chuck had taken many teams there, and Paul knew the pastor and his family. In 1973, Paul enrolled in the language school there, where he spent a few weeks learning Spanish.

For John, it was time in Honduras, El Salvador, and Nicaragua in 1974. He had an inquisitive mind and spent his time discovering the culture and history of that part of Central America. He learned to be comfortable in the cultures there, which was a blessing to him later in his life when he moved his family to St. Marten in the Caribbean for his medical schooling.

College Years

When it was time for Mark to head off to college, he chose Anderson College (now Anderson University) in Anderson, Indiana—the school where Chuck and I met. Chuck made Mark's trip to start his first semester there a memorable event. Just how many students go off to college their first year in a big private plane just for them? Mark did. Chuck had to pick up a team in Anderson to take to Mexico just as Mark was about to start his first semester, so we loaded Mark and his gear in the Convair, and off we went with Chuck flying. Mark settled into college life, choosing music as his major. Starting back in his high school years, Mark had encouraged his friends to call him by his first name, which was Charles, or Chuck. At college he only gave people the name Chuck, so from that time on he became another "Chuck."

Paul's turn for college came in 1975, and he too headed for Anderson College. He had already been involved in sound equipment. Taking his equipment with him in his van enabled him to start a little business called Natural Sound. He was able to use his talent and produce some money for his time in college.

John started his college career at Kansas State University in 1977 and soon discovered that wasn't the place for him. He later went to Anderson College, graduated from Indiana Wesleyan University, and got his MD from the American University of the Caribbean. That was quite an achievement.

The Family Grows

Chuck felt blessed to have three sons, and when they married, he was blessed to have three daughters too. Mark ("Chuck") announced his wedding plans for October 8, 1977, in Muskegon, Michigan, to Sue Bryson. It was easy to approve of his choice. She was a lovely girl, a good Christian, was graduating with a degree in nursing, and came from a wonderful family. Chuck and I were happy to add the first girl to our family of boys.

Grandpa Chuck

Paul and Dawn Lynch were married in Indianapolis on April 30, 1983. Paul too had found a lovely young Christian girl who fit in beautifully with our family. She also worked in the field of computer software as Paul did. She was another family blessing.

In 1988, John found his lovely bride, another wonderful Christian girl in the ER in Muncie, Indiana. They discovered they both had a love for serving people through medicine. He and Nancy Holland were married in her hometown of West Palm Beach, Florida, on October 16, 1988. Nancy totally supported him in his quest to be a doctor.

Families don't stop growing. Next the family was blessed by grandchildren. Mark and Sue added Heather, Erin, Bryson, and Allie to their family in Chicago. Paul and Dawn were blessed with Michael and John. And John and Nancy added Morgan, Martin, and Nicole to their family. What a fantastic group of nine wonderful grandchildren. With the marriage of Mark's daughters Heather to Nathan Peterson and Erin to Steve Voss and son Bryson to Lexie Conway came the possibility of great grandchildren. As of this writing, Heather and Nathan have brought Jude and Charlie, and Erin and Steve have added Isaiah to the family.

Though Chuck was not alive on this earth to welcome any of the additions after Michael, they are all the recipients of a great heritage because of the life he lived and the values he passed on. Chuck would swell with pride over his family now. They all love the Lord and have honored a Christian lifestyle. What more could any father want?

Chapter Eleven
PLAN BIG, HAVE FAITH, AND TRUST GOD

So everything was working out beautifully? No, not really. Somewhere in Chuck's spiritual journey from starting a church in 1952 to developing the ministry of Project Partner, the Lord showed him a principle for finding the way to accomplish his vision. It was the one-step-at-a-time principle. Beside Chuck's desk in the Project Partner office hung a huge poster with the words *Plan Big, Have Faith, and Trust God.* Those words must have inspired him to develop his own motto: "When you find a door shut, you don't give up; you search for another way to achieve your goal. You don't give in to adversity; you use it as a challenge to find another way."

Chuck said his motto came from the principle the Lord showed Joseph in the story recounted in Genesis 50:20. What is intended to harm a person or to stop a person is often used by the Lord in remarkable ways. He enables us to use problems and obstacles for good. Such was the case after Chuck established Project Partner, bought the airplane, and started working more extensively in missions activities.

Trying Times

Before Chuck purchased the plane in 1969 and while it was still a dream, he had gone to the Missionary Board of the Church of God to get approval. He wanted to help them develop more Christians committed to the Great Commission. He felt he could get more people interested in missions if they went to some of the mission fields and saw missions for themselves. He could show them the needs, the people, the native pastors, the missionaries, and what the Lord was doing.

Chuck thought he had the Missionary Board's approval. After he bought the plane, however, the board appeared to rethink the situation. What Chuck wanted to do was not the way missions were handled in those days. The board members said they wanted to "do missions" the way it had always been done. Those in leadership told him they were not endorsing his approach. Chuck's heart was only to help them further missions around the world. It was evident, however, that his way of helping was not acceptable to their way of thinking.

Up to this time, everything Chuck had done and all he knew about ministry was through the Church of God (Anderson, Indiana). He had grown up in a Church of God in Dayton, Ohio. He had graduated from Anderson College, a Church of God affiliated school, and he had married me, who also had grown up in a Church of God. He had gone from college to a position as associate pastor with Rev E. E. Kardatzke at the First Church of God in Wichita, Kansas. He had started the Pawnee Avenue Church of God and pastored it for eighteen years. All he knew was the Church of God, and he loved it.

Project Partner was going very well. People were making a commitment to leave their vocations and be a part of his team. Word was getting out across the Western Hemisphere of Project Partner's commitment to help churches in need anywhere and to provide wonderful opportunities to help them build the kingdom in their part of the world. Yet Chuck was called to Anderson to meet with the leaders of the Missionary Board time and time again to explain the purpose, the scope, and the future plans of Project Partner.

Chuck explained over and over that his purpose was to build the kingdom of God, not an organization, not Project Partner, not a church, and not a denomination. He wanted to do it in the way the Lord had directed him. He went to the meetings determined to cooperate in every way he could but continue with the purpose the Lord had given him. Historical perspective had shown Chuck he was simply ahead of his time, doing things no one had ever done before, so it was difficult for his vision to be accepted. After each meeting, all was fine for a little while, and then the board would call him to another meeting.

How many times in history have people who "think outside of the box" been challenged by those in authority? It is the ability to meet those challenges and still succeed that separates those with big plans from those with big accomplishments.

So what could Chuck do, given this challenge? He could sell the plane and forget the whole idea, or he could find another way to do what the Lord was telling him to do. He chose the latter, wondering what "another way" might be.

Moving On

Chuck had completed his type rating as captain, and his credentials were extensive.[1] It was time for Project Partner to expand. He encouraged

---

[1]

1948-49 Pvt. License Pilot Training, Anderson, IN
1955   Graduate School, Wichita State University
1966   Instrument Rating, Wichita State University, Yingling Aircraft, KS
1969   Commercial-Multi, Yingling Aircraft, Wichita, KS

Harold Perry and Loren Ralston, young men from his church, to earn their pilot's licenses and type ratings so they could fly with him. Joe Hooker, the best man at our wedding, had been a pilot during World War II, had his type rating, and was available to fly too, although he was pastoring a church in Oklahoma and was not available very often. Besides needing pilots, the ministry needed other support services. Chuck found a mechanic and hired him. Numerous people in the church helped with cleaning the plane and actually repainting and caring for it. In short, he had most of the resources he needed to move ahead with the ministry of Project Partner. His course was clear.

The lack of support from the Church of God Missionary Board remained an issue for Chuck. His respect for authority would not let him go against the board. His purpose was to serve the Lord and his church in spreading the message and the love of Christ wherever he could, but he was told directly by the board that they were looking at it through a different lens. Those in leadership eventually made it clear they didn't want anything to do with Project Partner. If Chuck was going to develop the mission outreach he had envisioned, he would have to find that "other way" soon to reach churches and people and get them interested in this new kind of ministry. He also had to keep the plane flying or get rid of it.

Requests continued to come in for work camps to various countries in the Caribbean. These were a blessing. Yet, there was always more need to keep the plane flying. One day Chuck said, "Donna, remember the good restaurant at the airport in Hutchinson? You know, where we had lunch when we were up there a couple of months ago? How would it be to fill the plane with anyone from the church who would like to go there for dinner on Sunday? We could have a great time over dinner, fly the plane up there and back to keep it current in flying, and make this a win-win situation."

We did it! And it worked. We enlisted people from our congregation to fly the forty or so miles from Wichita to Hutchinson, Kansas, twice a month for Sunday dinner at their nice airport restaurant. The 30-minute flight each way would keep the plane active, the people would

1969	Type Rating Convair, 240-340-440, Texas International, Dallas, TX
1976	Cert. F-27, Hughes Airlines, Phoenix, AZ
1977	Cert. Church Mgt., Dallas, TX
1977	Special Administration Mgt., San Bernardino, CA
1979	Advanced Adm. Management Training

pay $5 each, which was enough to cover the cost of the gasoline, and we would make a great excursion out of it. This idea worked for over a year and was a treat for everyone. It enabled Chuck to keep the plane active between mission trips and while he waited for the Lord to show him his next step in ministry.

Work Camps

Since Project Partner was not limited to ministry within the Church of God, Chuck began to reach out aggressively to other churches and groups. He honored the Church of God Missionary Board by not going against them. Instead, he went around them.

In 1970, Chuck began a work camp program. These "short-term mission trips," as they were later called, were a new idea for people who wanted to "do something" for the Lord. He started in Wichita with pastors whom he had met over the past twenty years. It wasn't long before he was taking the First Evangelical Free Church in Wichita to Mexico to build a church. He transported University Baptist and Immanuel Baptist to work in Nicaragua. Central Christian Church loaded the plane with their people for service in Guatemala.

When the massive earthquake hit Nicaragua in 1972, Chuck immediately enlisted people from every church he could to go and help in this time of need and reconstruction. Taking a reporter from the Wichita newspaper with him gave great press coverage and enabled Chuck to reach out to more churches across Kansas. He found workers from the Christian churches, the Methodist churches, the Presbyterian churches, Mennonites, Baptist, and many others. It was exciting to meet these people and work with them. They were open, they wanted to help, and they would assist in locating others who would also get involved. God was expanding Chuck's vision, plus developing precious relationships across denominational lines.

In 1975 the General Assembly of the Church of God chose to recognize Project Partner as a para-mission group, giving it status in working with the Church of God. This recognition was a blessed change from the previous times. It gave Project Partner a position of affiliation that would benefit the Church of God's missionary outreach far into the future.

Interestingly enough, the delay in acceptance by the Church of God had an unintended benefit (like Joseph's story). During this period of time, Chuck developed a clearer vision of expanding the kingdom of

God. It included not only the Church of God but many other churches throughout the country that were also accepting a new vision of missions for the world. Project Partner took teams from Indianapolis, Louisville, Birmingham, Phoenix, St. Louis, Chicago, Akron, Denver, Houston, Minneapolis, Lexington, Tulsa, Kansas City, Dayton, Morehead, Youngstown, Fort Wayne, Detroit, Washington, and Marion (Illinois). But more importantly, the Lord opened a new door: the door of working with many different evangelical churches across the United States.

By this time, Chuck's vision of the kingdom of God and the oneness of God's people was etched into the minds and hearts of the Project Partner team as well as in the hearts of his congregation and many others across the country. Chuck understood the message of Jesus Christ is always the same. It never changes. But the methods change continually. What works one time doesn't work the next time. What is the best way at one time is hampered by tradition in later years. One door closed doesn't mean it is time to quit. It means finding another way, another door. Project Partner's work camps in the early 1970s were the forerunner of short-term mission trips that would be offered by many other agencies and denominations in the years to come. They accomplished a tremendous amount of good for the Christians as well as non-Christians in many countries, including Peru, Panama, Barbados, El Salvador, Honduras, Belize, Haiti, Grenada, Trinidad, Nicaragua, Guatemala, and Mexico. They enabled many local churches and ordinary Christians to take giant steps in reaching people for Christ.

By 1989, approximately 120,000 people were short-term missionaries to places around the world. By 1998, the number had grown to 450,000. It was 1 million in 2003 and 2.2 million in 2006. How many will there be in 2012? What explosive growth from an idea sent from the Lord to a man who was ready and willing to tackle the impossible.

Chapter Twelve
ALL THINGS ARE POSSIBLE THROUGH CHRIST

Taking people on short-term mission trips to other countries in the Convair (and later a Fairchild 27) was spectacular. It certainly got people's attention. As with any new and innovative ministry, there were also roadblocks: people, systems, and authorities who had never conceived this way of serving the Lord. Chuck met these challenges head on.

Governmental regulations for the "aviation system" had always been a problem for all flights. It was mainly the regulatory agencies that had authority over the use of the 40-passenger planes. Chuck had to deal with the Civil Aviation Board (CAB), the Federal Aviation Authority (FAA), the Treasury Department, and Immigration and Customs. Back in 1969, commercial airlines were assigned routes by the CAB. They could not choose where they wanted to fly nor how often. They were told by the authorities what their routes would be. Likewise, Project Partner was subject to their control.

Chuck went to Washington to see how he would be able to fly the Convair for mission trips. When the CAB officials heard he wanted to pick up passengers in Indianapolis or St. Louis or Birmingham or wherever else he need to do so to go whenever he had a work camp project scheduled, they actually laughed at him. Impossible. He had to find another way.

Because Wichita was the center of aviation with Boeing, Cessna, Beech, and Lear aircraft factories, Chuck was able to find a good attorney who understood the problem. He and Chuck, working together, found a way to do what Chuck needed. It was to fly under CAB's Part 91, which was basically a club arrangement. Everyone who wanted to go with a team joined "the club" and simply paid a share of expenses. Chuck then went back to Washington to plead his case using "the club" concept. He presented this method to the CAB, and they agreed it would work. He won that one.

He then located a young pilot at Gulf Coast Bible College in Houston, Texas, who had his commercial and instrument licenses and was ready to work for Ozark Airlines. When Chuck presented Project Partner's vision for overseas trips to him, he chose to come and fly for us. Don Shaver and Chuck made a good team. They poured over the FAA books to see how they could comply with all the demands and requirements. They wrote manuals concerning maintenance and procedures.

Whatever the FAA required, they found a way to satisfy it. But their solutions were not without cost or problems.

There was an interesting run-in with one FAA employee in Kansas City whom Chuck had to work with for many approvals. This individual told Chuck he didn't want him to fly and was going to see to it that he was grounded someday, someway. Fortunately this man didn't succeed, although he was always there monitoring Chuck's activities.

The Treasury Department and Immigration and Customs had issues with Chuck too. They had never had to work with a plane like Project Partner's either, so they didn't quite know how to handle Chuck when he left and reentered the United States. He was finally able to obtain an exemption status, since Project Partner was a "charitable and religious organization." After receiving that status, Chuck could come back into the country with only a minimal fee instead of the tremendous fees commercial carriers had to pay, which would have in all likelihood made the trips prohibitive.

Keeping the 40-passenger plane in the air, making it safe for people, dealing with the government agencies, obtaining permits in foreign countries for refueling, and handling all the requirements to enter and exit each country were major tasks. In 1971, Chuck took our family to see the first of the series of the "Airport" movies. In the story, there were many employees with their assigned jobs. Chuck just laughed as he realized that between the two of us and a couple of other people to help us, he was able to get all of those jobs done.

Modern-Day Abrahams

By 1973, Chuck and Project Partner had quite a team. He surely needed all of them, but how did he get so many? The Lord called them, and they came by faith. They were modern-day Abrahams who were willing to leave their homeland and go into a land they did not know in order to be obedient to the Lord's call upon their life. It was adventure for them. But it was more. It was also obedience to the call of God.

Chuck was fortunate to have the help of Dick and Francene Sanders in Marion, Illinois. Dick had flown for Trans World Airlines, later renamed TWA before it was acquired by American Airlines in 2001, as well as the Illinois Air National Guard. He and Fran packed up their family and moved to Wichita to help. Dick was a great pilot, and Fran helped as a flight attendant when their two little boys were able to go along.

Claude and Jan Ferguson from Alliance, Ohio, came to help too. They caught the vision. Claude, who had built many houses in Ohio, knew with his skills in construction, he could handle the work camp department. He and Jan, with their four children, also packed up and moved west to Wichita.

John and Betty Wren felt the Lord calling them to come and help, so they left Birmingham, Alabama, and joined the team. Following them were Chester and Patsy Lemmond from Alabama; Rev. Jim and Lois Comstock from Illinois; Rev. Dan and Betty Ann Harman from Kentucky; Brenda Barlow from Louisiana; Rev. Gayle and Alice Van Asdale from Missouri; Joy Wharton from Ohio; Greg and Gail Bratton along with Ricka Brady and Faith King from Indiana; Victor and Betty Demarest from Oregon; Hugo Moriera from Uruguay; and Norm Carr, Jeanne Cornelius, Chuck and Shirley Moore, David and Judy Lymer, Gene and Ruth Basquez, Milton and Norma Regnier, Harold Perry, Bobbie Feiring, and Loren and LeMoine Ralston, plus more from Kansas. They all believed in the ministry. These people left their jobs and came to work with Project Partner. How amazing is that?

Since Project Partner could not supply funds for their support, they found another way—they were willing and able to raise support from their home church, relatives, and friends so they could be in the Lord's work. They found a way. They were a part of the team. They chose adventure with God, and they got it. They came and were instrumental in helping Chuck realize his dream, which had also become theirs.

During our Wichita years from 1969 to 1979, the Lord supplied fantastic teams for us. We had a total of about a hundred on staff all together during that period. We were serving in over twenty-two countries in the Western Hemisphere with around twelve two-week mission trips or more each year. We had been able to respond and serve after earthquakes, hurricanes, and civil war. The Lord had enabled us to put missions in the hearts of over 5,000 people on those adventures with him from Mexico to Brazil, from Trinidad to Panama, and beyond.

The Idea Continues

Are there aviation and travel clubs today? Just go to the Internet and find hundreds of them. They will take you to any country and give you an exciting experience. Seems like the FAA realized this idea of Chuck's would work. Project Partner pioneered the concept, was a model, a prototype, enabling numerous groups to follow in our footsteps. Amazing.

Does the story end here? Not at all. These growing pains and breakthroughs were only the beginning. The Lord was giving Chuck Thomas many more new ideas and visions. Great adventures lay ahead. Adventures no one ever dreamed.

The Lord always has more for us, and his plans are often something we never would have thought of, something new.

Chapter Thirteen
UNEXPECTED ADVENTURES

"Hey, look at this newsletter I got in the mail today. It talks about a group in Kansas with a big airplane taking people to other countries. They even work in Mexico and Guatemala and other countries down there and build churches. Have you ever heard of such a thing?"

"No, not really. I wonder how they do it. Sounds interesting."

"Yes, and look here. They are taking a group to Panama in January to build a church down there. This could be exciting. I think I'll check it out."

"Yeah, and let me know too. I've always been interested in Panama and would like to see their great canal."

This conversation was apparently going on in hundreds of homes in the late 1960s. The interest in our ministry was spreading by word of mouth from church to church. News about those first trips to Panama, Mexico, Haiti, and Guatemala was creating excitement. People were hearing about this new way of working for the Lord and were telling their families and friends. Project Partner had created an excitement among people who loved the Lord and wanted to share with others. What was happening sounded like adventure, adventure with the Lord.

Our phone rang constantly. People were eager to know what the trips were like, where they could be going, and what the cost would be. Their enthusiastic response was exciting and an answer to our prayers. Something so foreign, so distant, and so unreal was actually possible. Project Partner was making it possible for just about anybody to say, "Here am I. Send me!" (Isaiah 6:8).

Trips were lining up to Guatemala, Nicaragua, Costa Rica, Panama, and Honduras as well as Jamaica, Haiti, Cayman, Trinidad, and many other islands in the Caribbean. They would be starting from various cities across the United States. Christians living everyday, ordinary lives saw what we were doing as a new way to serve the Lord through missions without committing their entire lives for months or years to the mission field.

Most of the trips came off smoothly with thousands of people experiencing the thrill of serving the Lord through helping others throughout the world. Hundreds of men and women went to serve the Lord in places they had never heard of. There were, however, a number of trips with some memorable moments that at the time were, well, downright frightening. Chuck certainly didn't dream of encountering any of them.

Nicaragua 1971

In December 1971, Nicaragua had a devastating earthquake. It struck Managua, a city of a half million people, killing more than thirty thousand while completely devastating the heart of the city. Misael Lopez, a leader of Nicaraguan A.M.E.N. (Associacion Misionero Evangelica Nacional) churches, heard about Project Partner and went to Guatemala City to meet Chuck, who was there at the time with a work camp team. Misael pleaded with Chuck to help his people in Managua. Chuck agreed to help, but he decided we first needed to see the devastation in Nicaragua before he committed to taking a team.

He and I caught the next plane to Managua and saw the terrible destruction and chaos, felt the tremors. Chuck knew he needed to see the president of Nicaragua, General Somoza, to obtain permission to bring supplies in and to handle the distribution. He tried to get an appointment, but he was repeatedly told it was impossible. Somoza was too busy to see him. Yet Chuck persisted because he knew he had to get General Somoza's permission. He was also convinced the distribution would only go like he wanted it to go if he worked directly with Rev. Misael and his teams at the church rather than just giving everything to the government. Misael would know the best use of all the materials and supplies as well as the best ways to help people.

Chuck's persistence paid off. General Somoza did meet with him and sent him to the Minister of Defense, who presented him with an official letter stating he had President Somoza's approval to come and go as he wished. With a miracle like this one, Chuck was no longer Reverend Chuck Thomas in the eyes of Misael Lopez and the Nicaraguan pastors. He was Doctor Thomas (a new way to earn a doctoral degree).

Chuck hurried home to recruit people from all across the U.S. to go with him to help rebuild homes, schools, and churches. In two weeks, with the help of the Wichita news media, Chuck had a team from Kansas who also responded as Isaiah with, "Here I am. Send me!" This Project Partner team and others who followed it helped hundreds of destitute people. Thousands were living under cardboard boxes or simply a cloth strung between two poles. These teams were consumed with helping the destitute, the hurting people, giving them love and hope, and rebuilding their homes, churches, and schools.

Chuck next contacted Gulf Coast Bible College, in Houston, Texas, and offered to take the school choir to sing and encourage the people. The Nicaraguans' morale was at an all time low. He reasoned, what could bring them a moment's relief better than some beautiful inspirational music? They desperately needed to hear songs, put their faith back in God, and gain hope for the future. The college officials agreed. The choir went and put on several spectacular concerts in Central Park in Managua, the capital, right among the ruins and devastation, to an extremely receptive audience. The choir sang their American songs in English yet the people of Managua relished the music, the attention, and the obvious care and concern these young people had for them. Hundreds of hurting people came from under their cardboard boxes and their makeshift lodgings, crawling out of those piles of rubble to hear music again in their souls.

At the end of the first year after the earthquake, President Somoza called Chuck into his office. He told him how much Spain, Mexico, England, the United States, and other countries had helped. He then went on to say:

> I realize your monetary investment in our country has not been nearly as great as these I've mentioned, but I am expressing appreciation to you and your organization for the fact that you brought us people. Our people needed people. You are the only organization who brought in people, planeloads of people, to be with our Nicaraguans in their time of great despair.
>
> I have announced a motto for our country for the next year. I have called it "The Year of Reconstruction." However, because of the significant contribution you and Project Partner have made, I have added the words "and hope." This coming year will be known as "The Year of Reconstruction and Hope." Thank you, Reverend Thomas.

An Extra Passenger

A bit later, on one of the trips returning from Nicaragua, Chuck experienced a frightening incident. It was during a time when there were several reports of airplanes being hijacked. On this particular trip, Chuck and Dick Sanders had just taken off from the airport in Managua when Bobbie, the flight attendant, rushed to the cockpit to tell Chuck somebody was hiding in the galley.

Chuck immediately called the tower to talk to aviation control and tell them he thought he had a stowaway on board. He was ordered to return to the field, where he would be met by airport officials. Chuck had to burn off fuel for about 30 minutes before he could land, as the plane had full tanks and was too heavy for a safe landing. When he finally could land, he quickly taxied to the terminal. The airport police were right there and raced up the steps and to the back of the plane. There they discovered a teenager hiding behind the cooler.

This young man had seen the teams in action with the hurting people in Managua and felt their compassion. His parents had been killed during the earthquake, and he wanted to go home with his new friends. He felt he could have a future with them, since he didn't have a home or any future in Nicaragua. Unfortunately, the government would not let this young man go with Chuck and the team, so they reached into their pockets and gave him some money. Chuck then arranged for this young stowaway to go to Rev. Misael. Of course, Chuck checked on him on subsequent trips.

Guatemala 1972

Chuck and I had our three boys on board in January 1972 for our family's first trip to Mexico and Guatemala. The trip was scheduled to include four days in Mexico City for the Christian World Conference; a day in Cuernavaca, Mexico, to see how Christianity was viewed there; and six days in Guatemala City. Our main focus for this Eyewitness Crusade (the ministry name we had given to this type of trip) was Guatemala. We would be meeting with pastors and churches from the Caribbean side to the Pacific side to encourage them and learn what God was doing in this country.

It was a full flight to Mexico City, and it was certainly an eye-opener for those never having traveled outside the United States. After the conference and the day in Cuernavaca, our next stop was Guatemala City. Unbeknown to us, trouble was ahead. There were thunderstorms in the flight path, but that was not the only trouble. As the wind began bumping us around, creating concern and uneasiness, a major problem developed. The airport in Guatemala City radioed it was closed and we could not land there.

What were Chuck's alternatives? There were only two other airports in the whole country of Guatemala—Puerto Barrios, east on the Caribbean coast, and Puerto San Jose, south on the Pacific Coast. Puerto San Jose was closer, but it was a military base and not open to civilian planes. Chuck conferred with Jerry, his copilot, and they felt Puerto Barrios was too far away. So they turned the plane south toward Puerto San Jose, the military base.

By then it was dark, and threatening clouds surrounded us. As we neared Puerto San Jose, try as he could, Chuck couldn't get the tower radio to respond. He couldn't figure out what the problem was. Chuck and his copilot could see only one little light down on the ground, but it was not enough for them to locate the runway. The gage showed they were running low on fuel. Chuck realized he was out of alternatives. He had to either find the runway or go over and land on the beach. The beach would be dangerous and do damage to the plane. It was an alternative, but certainly not a good one. He and Jerry chose to try to find the runway.

Peering through the darkness, they were finally able to locate the runway and proceeded to make the final approach. Jerry kept calling, trying to get the tower to respond. It was silent, deathly silent. Even though Chuck and he could hardly see and were praying all the time, they were able to ease the wheels onto the runway. The Lord provided a safe and an uneventful landing. They certainly breathed a prayer of thanks to the Lord for keeping them from what could have been a major disaster.

Ahead was a small light over in the distance on the right, so they started taxiing the plane toward it. Suddenly two military trucks came speeding up and stopped right in front of the plane. "What's this?" Chuck thought. "Where have they been all the time?" He quickly lowered the steps and sent Luz Gonzales, his interpreter, down to see what we could do. When Luz saw the soldiers with automatic rifles and fixed bayonets, he ran double time back up the steps. Chuck said he never saw anybody run up those steps as fast as Luz did.

Chuck was the captain, so it was his responsibility to handle the crisis. First he put on his Captain cap (a sign of authority), and then he went down the steps. The commander was waiting for him. Chuck told him our plane was a church plane, and it was on its way to Guatemala City. Those on board were just people from the United States coming to see Guatemala City, but the plane had been prevented from landing at its planned destination because of the storm.

The commander wasn't convinced. During the past decade, there had been many hijackings in Latin America, making him extremely skeptical about any plane landing there, especially one landing on such a dark night. He thought he was handling another hijacking. He was immediately ready to deal with the situation, and with military force. He commanded our team off the plane and ordered them to stand under the right wing. Chuck asked me to take two of the soldiers with their automatic rifles on board so they could search the plane. Those soldiers did search it thoroughly from front to back, finally deciding everything was okay. Chuck didn't know at the time what they were looking for, but later he realized it was probably drugs. After the two soldiers reported to the commander that there was nothing of consequence on board, the commander relaxed and decided to help "these foreigners." The soldiers put their guns away, and the atmosphere was suddenly much friendlier.

Chuck told the commander he wanted to get to a phone and have a bus come from Guatemala City to pick up our people. The commander, knowing it would take two hours for a bus to get there, invited everyone to go into the hanger to wait. He told Chuck to tell all the passengers to gather their bags and the ladies to climb in the back of the military trucks so they could be taken to the hanger. It was simply a hanger—no chairs, no tables, and no food either. We had planned to eat dinner in Guatemala City, and we were hungry. Since there was no food in sight, everyone brought out stashes of cheese and crackers, nuts, cookies, candy, oranges, apples, and bananas. When we started sharing with each other, it was like the loaves and fishes in Jesus' time. Our group even shared with the soldiers. The Lord blessed us with everyone having enough to eat and some left over.

The soldiers were quite nice to us. Since we had two hours to wait for the bus, our group made a big circle, invited the soldiers to join us, and, as Christians often do when they have time on their hands, we sang, had prayer, and shared our thoughts on the day. When the bus finally arrived, I took the group on to Guatemala City and the hotel. Chuck, Jerry, and our son Mark stayed behind and brought the plane up the next morning.

The rest of the trip went smoothly and as planned, but this group would never forget the extraordinary night experience in Puerto San Jose.

Mexico 1974

Within five years after the founding of Project Partner, Chuck and his crews were flying teams from several different cities in the U.S. all over Central America and the Caribbean. In 1974 Richard Nixon was president, Watergate was erupting, and the world was at the beginning of what would become known as the Oil Crisis as gasoline skyrocketed from around $.50 a gallon to almost $2.00 a gallon. There was talk of conservationism across the world.

On one particular trip to Mexico, Chuck had one of Project Partner's crews flying a team of thirty-six. They had just built a church in Tecpan, Guatemala, and were returning home feeling so blessed for what they had been able to accomplish. Chuck was in his office in Wichita monitoring their return flight, as was his custom. His phone rang, telling him the plane was in trouble. They always fueled at Merida, Mexico, on the Yucatan Peninsula, and they had permission to do so for this trip too. However, some Mexican officials had changed their minds. They felt the United States was not being fair to them when they flew into U.S. cities. The U.S. government would sell them only enough fuel to get back to Mexico and refused to fill their tanks. The Mexican officials considered this tactic an insult, so they decided they were going to get even by refusing to fuel the Convair this time. The crew was informed that until the United States changed its policy and would fuel Mexican plane tanks full, the Convair was going to be kept in a hostage situation. It was inconceivable. This small group of ordinary U.S. citizens on a mission trip to help people in Central America was put into the position of pawns on the political chess board by some Mexican officials trying to change U.S. government policy.

Chuck immediately called Enrique Cepeda, who was living in Mexico City at that time, and told him the problem. Enrique got busy with his friends and their contacts in Mexico City. With the Lord's help, they were able to talk to the right people. In the meantime, Chuck called his friends to pray. He knew he could depend on the Lord to get him out of this situation. Sure enough, the Lord used Enrique to pull off a miracle. After five hours, the Mexican officials agreed to let the plane be fueled, and the team headed on to New Orleans and home. Chuck talked for weeks about the Lord again getting the plane out of a mess.

The Guatemala Earthquake 1976

In response to the challenge a Guatemalan pastor gave Chuck in 1971 when he asked for help with a church building, Chuck had been sending numerous teams from all across the U.S. to Guatemala. The teams had built some forty churches: from Puerto Barrios on the east coast to as far west as the mountains around Quezaltenango, from the north around Coban to as far south as Puerto San Jose on the Pacific coast. Then came February 4, 1976. Guatemala had an unbelievable earthquake.

Because of his experience with the Nicaragua earthquake of 1971, Chuck was ready to help. He immediately caught the next plane to see for himself what the damage was and what was needed. It wasn't long before he was on the phone reporting to me about this quake. It was every bit as bad as the one in Nicaragua. Preparations needed to start immediately to recruit teams to come at once and help. There in Guatemala he was able to enlist help from Beech Aviation in Guatemala City because of his affiliation with Beech Aircraft (now Ratheon in Wichita). With Beech's help, he arranged for critical supplies to be flown into remote areas using roads for landing strips.

Next Chuck was able to send me some slides of the tremendous disaster the earthquake had caused so they could be shown at churches in Wichita. The churches we had been working with were anxious to know the extent of the damage. As the people saw the pictures and because they had left their hearts in Guatemala from previous trips with Project Partner, many were eager to be a part of the recovery process by signing up to go or providing equipment and funds. The staff at Project Partner also sent out a special newsletter across the country to enlist teams from various cities and churches. They wanted to be ready for the first trips as soon as Chuck returned.

One church in Wichita in particular was impressed when its people heard the news that every Presbyterian church in Guatemala was either destroyed or severely damaged. The church was having a missions banquet in a couple of days, so I was able to show them the slides. They determined to do what they could to help. The church, Eastminster Presbyterian, decided to send its pastor and two elders to meet Chuck in Guatemala to assess the damage.

When the Eastminster team returned and reported to the Session, the Elders decided to reduce the church's building project, in process of being approved, from a $500,000 expansion to $150,000. In addition, the church would raise $180,000 to replace every one of the destroyed Presbyterian churches in Guatemala. The Session called a special meeting to present the plan, called Project Light, to the congregation. The people voted unanimously, yes unanimously, in favor of rebuilding every one of the churches in Guatemala.

This church's response was just an example of the response of churches Chuck had been working with from Florida to California.

Project Partner had built a great reputation of service and help. People knew the kind of man Chuck Thomas was; they were impressed with all the staff and workers. They also responded to the purpose Chuck had to be a servant of the Lord to whomever and wherever as the need arose. People lined up to go. Every three weeks for the next nine months, the plane was loaded with a new team to work for two weeks in Guatemala, rebuilding churches and schools, serving the homeless and hungry, and doing whatever else was needed.

"Thumbs Up!"

Here are Chuck's thoughts on some of the ministry adventures of these years, written by him and published in the Project Partner newsletter ONWARD.

"THUMBS UP!"
By Charles Thomas, 1979

"THUMBS UP!" has been a way of life for people involved with Project Partner through the years. The signal or sign given by someone with his hand clinched into a fist with the thumb partially up is used by many people for many different purposes, but generally it simply means "READY."

In the cockpit of an airplane, the captain gives the "THUMBS UP" signal and the co-pilot responds with the words of "GEAR UP" and proceeds to activate the landing gear lever.

To the people of Project Partner the word "READY" has meant go to the scene of the action immediately. When a dreaded earthquake struck Guatemala City in 1976, I caught the next plane out to assess the situation. I contacted Donna by ham radio relaying to her the situation as I found it. Her immediate response was "READY." She put into action the plans which we at Project Partner had made months and years before.

Project Partner's "READY" response began with the shipping of an ambulance, a dump truck, a small bulldozer and provision which consisted of food, tents, and clothing which were flown to Guatemala City in our large airplane. The "READY" signal was answered by paramedics, doctors, nurses, and laborers "READY" to help during this time of disaster.

When hurricane Fifi struck the coast of Honduras back in 1974, Project Partner joined in with many U.S. Air Force planes to deliver food, clothing, and medical supplies to a hurting people. I recall how beautiful the coordination of the operation was when a Christian doctor met our plane and utilized the medical supplies which we had delivered.

Nicaraguans for years have been a depressed people under the harsh dictatorship of Anastasio Somoza. When the earthquake of 1972 hit Nicaragua, the poor people were totally helpless to take care of themselves. Again the people of Project Partner responded "READY." In spite of President Somoza's iron rule, we prayed, asking for guidance, and then stepped out on faith. President Somoza gave Project Partner permission to land its large aircraft and deliver men, women, and the necessary supplies to help rebuild churches and homes for the people of Nicaragua.

When medical needs were made known to Project Partner from several countries, we sounded the "READY" alert again. A Christian couple donated their own personal yacht to be converted into a medical clinic. Hundreds of people found "SEA ANGEL" "READY" to minister to their medical needs.

You do what you must! If at all possible, the people of Project Partner respond "READY" whether in Lebanon, Mexico, Guatemala, Grenada, Jamaica, Barbados, Peru, Colombia, or China. Times change. However, the needs are ever before us, and Project Partner continues to meet those needs.

Chapter Fourteen
LEARNING TO GIVE

It was certainly a "thumbs up" and "ready" time to go further with this ministry. The Lord was blessing our endeavors and giving Chuck more ideas and visions of what could be done to share the message of Jesus Christ with those who had never heard it. I called his lifestyle "thinking outside of the box." He called it "adventures in taking the good news to the world." Today it would be called "missional living."

The Pawnee Avenue Church was doing well. It had changed from a good church to a missional church—missional in every sense of the word. A sending church. Sending its people out on missions whenever and wherever the Lord was leading. The congregation was totally behind all of Chuck's endeavors. They were helping, they were enlisting others, they were praying, and they were supporting all these activities. They had a vision for the lost and were eager to be a part of everything they could. No longer was it an ordinary church. It had a mission heart. It was a church on mission with and for the Lord.

The *Sea Angel* and the Tootsie Rolls

One afternoon in 1973, Chuck received a call from a man in Alabama named Ray Helms. Ray said he had a forty-seven-foot yacht he thought could be very useful in mission work. Having heard about Project Partner and having asked the Lord for guidance, he felt he should approach Chuck with his dream.

Chuck was quick to think of all kinds of possibilities. He could see ways to use the yacht as an evangelism tool. He was aware of peoples living in remote areas of Central America who knew nothing of Jesus Christ. They could be reached with the gospel via a boat up their rivers and along their coasts. He also saw it as a way to help them with their need for medical care. It could be just the place for doctors to serve and also to show them the love of God. He was filled with excitement about all the possibilities as we headed to Titusville, Florida, to meet with Ray.

Ray Helms seemed just as excited as Chuck was about the yacht being used in ministry. Here was an exceptional resource with all kinds of possibilities. There was a place for a doctor's examination room, bedrooms for a crew, storage area for Bibles and medicines, a waiting area for visitors, plus a kitchen and eating space. Together Chuck and Ray decided to name the boat *Sea Angel*. They wanted it to be an angel of love and mercy wherever it was located. Ray was experiencing the joy of giving.

Ray said he was willing to get the boat to whatever location Chuck would choose. Having been all over Central America and the Caribbean, Chuck's thoughts turned to Guatemala. A good river might be the Rio Dulce, which winds its way to the coast and empties into the Caribbean at Livingston. Rio Dulce originates in Lake Izabal making it a good place to serve as a base of operations.

Chuck felt the first step would be to go to Guatemala and check out this river. He flew to Guatemala City, where he consulted with a cultural anthropologist at the University of Guatemala as to where he thought the best location would be. The anthropologist agreed the Rio Dulce would be a great river to use, a good location in the country, and the people in that area would welcome the medical help as well as be open to Christianity. Chuck then secured the service of a Mission Aviation Fellowship (MAF) pilot to fly him over the area. (MAF is a Christian organization providing airplane service in remote areas of the world.) It was certainly a jungle and mountainous area, but the winding path of the Rio Dulce, plus the accessibility of Lake Izabel, looked just like what Chuck had in mind.

Chuck's next step was to take a bus from Guatemala City to Livingston, the country's main sea port on the Caribbean, to check it and the river out personally. In Livingston he hired a guide with a dugout canoe. Leaving his luggage in a hotel for what he thought was a short trip, he grabbed only his raincoat and a package of Tootsie Rolls in case he got hungry. Off they went.

There Chuck was, with a guide he didn't know, in a dugout canoe on a remote river in Guatemala when suddenly a storm came up. The storm quickly became very strong and was filling the canoe with spraying water. The guide chose to dock the canoe at the next village along the river, and then he suddenly disappeared. As Chuck waited, trying to decide what to do next, he noticed the natives of the village coming out of their huts, carrying bags and supplies and heading up a path toward the nearby mountain in what seemed to be an effort to get away from the storm. Being a pilot, Chuck quickly recognized the storm was rapidly becoming a hurricane.

Chuck also realized something else. The people of the village were heading the wrong way. They were going right into the eye of the storm. They needed to find shelter lower down rather than at a higher elevation.

Not able to talk with them in their language, Chuck joined them in their journey. As soon as he could, he used the Tootsie Rolls he had brought with him as an enticement to get them to follow him to a safer place. He showed them one, unwrapped it, and took a bite. That caught their attention. He offered each of them one, and a trust level began developing. Next Chuck took the lead, and they followed him because they liked those Tootsie Rolls. By sign language and Tootsie Rolls, he led them to a safe place away from the eye of the storm.

When the storm had passed, the Indians chose to go on to the top of the mountain, where they had their own gods to worship. Chuck was left alone again, this time, unsure where the path was to get him back to the river and civilization. There were so many paths, and they all looked alike. He knew the snakes in this part of Guatemala were so deadly a person would die within thirty minutes after being bitten. He set out on a path that seemed right, trusting God for safety and direction. Whenever he met native Indians on the trail, he would get their attention by giving them a Tootsie Roll. By sign language, he would then ask how to get to the river. He traveled on foot for two days and spent two nights lying on top of large rocks and praying for a way out of the dense jungle.

On the third day, he finally came into a clearing. There was a little cornfield and ahead was what looked like a small chapel. Walking on, he discovered it was a Catholic church. Inside he saw a priest, and to his amazement, the priest could speak English. The priest also had a ham radio, making it possible for Chuck to call me back in the United States and to confirm his whereabouts.

The most interesting part of the story was when Chuck arrived back at the port in Livingston. The port captain gave him the papers he needed to use the Rio Dulce for *Sea Angel*, and then he looked closely at Chuck. "Sir," he said, "were you out in the midst of the storm?" As Chuck affirmed he had been, the port captain continued. "Some Indians were in here, and they were talking about a tall white man who had led them to safety during the storm. They thought the man was a god because he had provided the protection they needed."

Giving Health and Hope

Chuck and his team eventually got the boat functioning on Lake Izabal, and it became a source of health and hope. When the people in the area and surrounding region were in need, they would get in their dugout canoes and row over for help. The name *Sea Angel* seemed just right, as it was serving hundreds there in a remote area both medically and spiritually. Chuck recruited Gladys Smith, a nurse, to live on *Sea Angel*. He recruited Victor and Betty Demarest to captain the boat. Numerous doctors spent either one or two weeks on board, attending to the needs of the native Indians. Chuck even arranged for work teams to build a clinic at one of the villages on the shore of Lake Izabal. He also recruited Hugo Moriera, a native of Uruguay, to be the much-needed evangelist and to establish a church.

After the church had gained strength and had a native pastor, Chuck chose to move *Sea Angel* and the crew on to Nicaragua. It too was a profitable location, providing much needed medical help and producing a church on the Rio Escondido. Next was Costa Rica, where *Sea Angel* worked the Caribbean coast around Limon for a couple of years. The last location was the Roatan Islands of Honduras. There Chuck sent teams for a clinic to be built at Oak Harbor.

In 1982, Chuck ended up giving the clinic to World Gospel Mission, as they had missionaries at Oak Harbor. The *Sea Angel* was by then needing major repairs, making it time, in Chuck's mind, to move on to other ways of serving these people. He was well acquainted with the third chapter of Ecclesiastes, knowing there is a time for everything: "A time to keep and a time to throw away" (verse 6). *Sea Angel* was sold to some fishermen in Honduras and soon was lost in a hurricane.

Learning the Principle of Giving It Away

By 1977, the operation of Project Partner was going along quite well and was recognized by many. Chuck had a good staff that had come from across the U.S. Great excitement was generated from the teams going on short-term mission trips and all the new experiences they encountered. Teams had helped significantly after the two major earthquakes in Nicaragua and Guatemala and the hurricane in Honduras. Yet Chuck had a divine discontent in his heart. He felt he needed to be a better leader.

Campus Crusade was scheduled to have a citywide meeting in Kansas City called World Thrust. The director of the event was Dr. Larry Poland. Chuck thought he might learn something from this meeting, so we went. Right after the evening session, we sought out Dr. Poland and invited him to the ice cream shop.

"Larry," Chuck started, "we have a small mission agency, but we are taking hundreds of people throughout the Western Hemisphere on

114

short-term mission trips. We've helped with earthquakes and hurricanes. We've built churches, schools, clinics, and even hangers for MAF (Missionary Aviation Fellowship). However, I don't think we are very well organized. Surely there must be a better way to run our organization. Do you have time to help us?"

Larry did even better than Chuck expected. He went back to Campus Crusade headquarters, which was at Arrowhead Springs in California at that time, and talked to Dr. Bill Bright, the founder and president of Campus Crusade for Christ, a renowned Christian organization serving youth in colleges and universities in numerous countries around the world. Dr. Bright and Dr. Poland then invited Chuck and me to come there for two weeks, even offering to cover our expenses during the time there. They would work with us, find our strengths and weaknesses, and help us develop Project Partner for the next level of its ministry.

Of course, Chuck accepted their offer, and both Dr. Poland and Dr. Bright gave us tremendous help. We wrote missions statements, short- and long-term goals, strategy, and plans. We worked on purpose, donor relations, marketing, and a lot more. It was difficult for us to imagine Campus Crusade giving its valuable time to help a young, relatively unknown organization, but this is exactly what happened. They freely shared everything they had.

Chuck learned a tremendous amount during those two weeks, and it was extremely valuable. The key thing he learned, however, was to give everything away. He was to build the kingdom of God, not an empire for himself. He was to promote the gospel of Jesus Christ, not Project Partner. From then on, Chuck had the joy of giving. The principle of giving it away led him to give the clinic on Lake Izabal in Guatemala to the missionaries there. It led him to give the clinic at Oak Harbor to World Gospel Mission. Thanks to Campus Crusade, he was able to stay focused on his purpose of helping and serving and not go into the business of building an empire for personal gain or for Project Partner. He was indebted to these great men, Bill Bright and Larry Poland, and their organization for investing in him.

Investing in What Lasts

The principle of giving it away also caused Chuck to invest in many new ventures. One was the life of a young Mexican he had met on one of the short-term mission trips. Abel Reyna had finished his education at La Buena Tierra in Saltillo, but he had a deep longing to be a medical doctor. He had no money, of course. Chuck believed in him and helped him earn his medical degree. He became a well-known urologist in Saltillo, Mexico. One of his sons followed in his footsteps as well.

Chuck saw another young man he felt led to invest in, this one in Nicaragua. He was working with Pastor Misael Lopez. Miguel Pinell was just what the communist government of Ortega wanted in the revolution. Chuck had observed his abilities and commitment when he worked with him after the earthquake in Managua. Miguel had already been in prison twice because he refused to follow the communist doctrine. In order to give this young, twenty-one-year-old a future out of the reach of the communists, Chuck brought Miguel to our house in Ohio in 1983. He sent him to language school and helped him stay on the right path. Miguel went on to Warner Southern College for his degree in pastoral studies. He presently has a tremendous ministry in Honduras reaching thousands of people for the Lord as the national leader with Heart to Honduras.

Still in the giving mode, Chuck purchased a van for a missionary in Mexico. He said, "They need one. We can get one. Let's do it." He was also instrumental in obtaining a car for a young woman missionary in Saltillo, Mexico. Later we had the privilege of attending her wedding at La Buena Tierra.

Chuck felt blessed that the Lord enabled him to see needs and address them one way or another. He had learned the joy of giving. He also made Project Partner an organization that would continue to give, help, and enable the Lord's present-day disciples to build the kingdom of God far into the future.

Conventions, Another Challenge

Missions conventions were relatively new in those days. Chuck envisioned one where large groups of people would get excited about missions. Why not? He organized a couple of them in Wichita and later in Middletown, Ohio. Bringing in key leaders sparked attendance and added to the enthusiasm. People looked forward to hearing from Dr. Ben Jennings, Executive Director of the U.S. Center for World Missions; Judy Douglas and Dr Larry Poland, two of Bill Bright's key executives at Campus Crusade; and Dr. Robert Coleman from Asbury Seminary. He also brought in renowned leaders in the Church of God: Dr. Dale Oldham, Dr. Arlo Newell, Dr. R Eugene Sterner, Dr. Sam Hines, Dr. Ross Minkler, Dr. David Grubbs, Dr. Milton Grannum,

Dr. Maurice Bergquist, and Dr. Max Gaulke, along with numerous others. Those were unique events, well attended, with more and more people catching the vision and picking up the mantel to help change the world for Jesus Christ.

The Lord Has His Plans ... A Future

Although Chuck gained great satisfaction from these accomplishments, he was always looking ahead to see what else the Lord had in store for him to do. He cherished the words in Jeremiah 29:11, "For I know the plans I have for you..." His response of saying "why not?" to ideas always led him on to even more new and strange adventures. So what would be his next adventure?

Chapter Fifteen
CHANGES AND TRANSITIONS

"Would Rev. Chuck Thomas please come forward."

A surprise. Right there in the middle of the evening service, during the annual camp meeting at Camp Fellowship, Chuck was called out. He made his way to the front and up on the platform, not knowing why he had been called forward.

The speaker continued, "Chuck, you have been chosen as 'Pastor of the Year' for 1972 by the Kansas Assembly."

As was his nature, Chuck thanked the speaker, accepted the plaque, and turning to the congregation, said, "This is a special honor, and I greatly appreciate it. I don't know if I have done anything exceptional, but I give the Lord all the credit for what he has allowed me to do. Maybe you are honoring me because I've been around here so long." That brought a good laugh. The honor was a sign that change was ahead once again.

Classroom Without Walls

Somewhere in this timeframe of his life, Chuck came up with another idea to possibly transform the lives of others. His challenge was to help college students get a heart for missions. He headed to Warner Southern College in Lake Wales, Florida, a Church of God college. There he presented his idea of taking students to other countries for a semester's work in anthropology and cross-cultural studies. They would actually take the curriculum of one of the classes at the Warner Southern and apply it in the context of the culture in another country. He called it Classroom Without Walls. President Leroy Fulton listened to Chuck's proposal and decided to try it.

The first session of Classroom Without Walls was in Guatemala in 1973. Chuck enlisted his Mexican pastor friend, Enrique Cepeda, to guide the team of eighteen students and keep them on track. They worked with two of the universities in Guatemala City and researched lifestyles in various villages. It was very well received both in Guatemala and back home in Florida. The next year Chuck also recruited Grant and Carol Milikan, who had recently graduated from Anderson College, to take a team to Mexico, then one to Nicaragua, and later one to Germany. This new idea of Chuck's was the beginning of college students doing some of their studies overseas. It was a great idea and has caught on everywhere.

The Fairchild 27

By 1976, Project Partner had taken numerous short-term missions teams in the Convair to more than twelve different countries. The airplane needed constant attention to keep it in shape for these trips. Chuck had a full-time aviation mechanic, and he also took the Convair to Dallas for regular check-ups with Delta mechanics. When a major problem arose with one of the engines as a team was returning home from Central America, Chuck decided to reevaluate the status of the plane. It was old when he bought it. It had served the ministry very well. Perhaps it was time to upgrade.

Chuck started a search for a better plane. The search led him to a Fairchild 27 turbo prop. These engines made quite an improvement over the Convair with its reciprocal engines. Chuck brought his team together to make the decision. The bus had cost $3,500. The Convair had cost $35,000. This plane added another zero, making the price $350,000. Again it was money he didn't have, yet Chuck believed in Hebrews 11:1: "Faith is being sure of what we hope for and certain of what we do not see." With confidence in the Lord, he and his pilots bought the plane, sold the Convair, and went to Phoenix to get their pilot's type rating for the F 27.

In the next two years, Chuck was busy raising the funds to pay for the new plane as he and his staff put it to work for more ministry trips. But then major changes in aviation began to happen. The FAA changed some of its regulations. No longer were commercial airlines confined to specific routes. The CAB went out of existence, enabling airlines to choose their flights and their cities to serve. As the airlines expanded their outreach, they were also able to expand their market. This expansion brought about lowered prices. Chuck discovered his teams could fly as cheaply or even cheaper on a commercial flight than they could with our own plane. Okay. Now it was time to sell the F 27 and go commercial.

The F 27 sold easily to a commuter company on the East Coast; however, this change wasn't the end of aviation for Chuck Thomas. He was a partner with a group flying a Cessna 210. In a couple of years, they purchased a Cessna 310 twin engine. These planes enabled him and the staff to go whenever and wherever to speaking engagements and appointments across the U.S.

A Year of Transitions

Four major things happened within the span of 1977 that would change the direction of Chuck's life. First, the house was empty, or so it seemed. No boys. They were grown and gone. It was difficult to accept, but our life at home would never be the same.

Second, the Pawnee church congregation chose to have a big celebration for our twenty-fifth anniversary of Chuck as its pastor. They put together a "This Is Your Life" party with the whole church participating. And did they ever work at it. It was fantastic. They had a big banquet on Saturday night that necessitated using the sanctuary, as it was the biggest place. This choice, however, meant taking out all the rows of pews, even though they were bolted down, and getting them back in place before services on Sunday morning.

The program was copied from the TV program by the same name. People who were important to Chuck and me were brought to the celebration. Chuck's mom from Ohio along with her sister Liz and brother-in-law were special guests. The Fischers, who befriended us when we were camping in Colorado and were key to our relationship with the many people there, were present there. My parents, who were living in Wichita, were also there and included on the program. Others came from as far as away as Nicaragua and Guatemala just for the celebration.

Phone calls from Chuck's previous pastors, Dr. Dale Oldham and Dr. Eugene Sterner from Anderson, were amplified for everyone to hear. Loren Ralston, one of our young men and also one of Project Partner's pilots, did a super job as emcee. The party planners were even able to capture the event on videotape, which was in its infancy in 1977. It was a wonderful time sharing memories for those twenty-five years of ministry. Many stories were told, but one of the funniest was of the young boy who, every time he saw Chuck, called him God. Chuck was always quick to tell the boy he had the wrong name for him.

The third major change in Chuck's life that year happened in December of 1977. Chuck resigned as pastor of the Pawnee Avenue Church. He had pastored there for twenty-five years. It was time to move on. Chuck had been planning for this time. He had brought Jerry Phillips in as an associate pastor first and then moved him up as co-pastor. Earlier in the year, he had made Jerry senior pastor. He wanted the church to have a smooth transition when the time came.

The twenty-five years with the Pawnee church family was over. We had left. But the first Sunday after the farewell party was difficult. Where would we go? Chuck didn't feel like he should go to either of the other two Church of God congregations in Wichita, so he decided we would go to three other churches—Central Christian for the early service, Eastminster Presbyterian for the eleven o'clock service, and University Baptist for the evening service. This approach was modified at times by including a fourth church in the mix with services at Asbury Methodist. Chuck was working with these four churches and their pastors through Project Partner, so it was easy to feel a part of them. His world was expanding again.

Since Chuck had developed a relationship with pastors of several denominations, it wasn't long before he set up regular breakfast meetings with them. It was a communion they all needed, enjoyed, and didn't have anywhere else. It was a rich pastors' fellowship.

The fourth change in Chuck's life was an even bigger one than leaving Pawnee. At the Project Partner Board of Directors meeting in the spring of 1978, Chuck was challenged to move the headquarters of the ministry to a more central location in the U.S. This took some prayer and study, as we had lived in Wichita for twenty-eight years. It was home, it was where our sons were born, we had many friends there, and we weren't looking for the trauma accompanied with moving. Yet Chuck saw this call to move, also, as a challenge he needed to respond to. Was it a new direction from the Lord? Sensing it was the Lord's will, Chuck accepted the challenge and set out to find the place the Lord had prepared.

He began to study the Bible belt, where most of the people came from who went on Project Partner mission trips. He realized southwest Ohio was somewhat in the center. So to check out the area and in order to be accepted by the churches there, Chuck spent a couple of weeks meeting with various pastors from Dayton to Cincinnati and all in between. He wanted their approval for having the ministry based there. Every one of them seemed excited about Project Partner being in their area, so the next step was to choose just where.

Chuck decided a location halfway between Dayton and Cincinnati would be a good place, since it was close to those two large airports. He found office space for rent in Middletown and a warm reception from the area pastors, so he decided to land there. He had quite a staff to move to Ohio. He chose to send one of Project Partner's families ahead to get things started. In July the rest of the team loaded their furniture and headed those 800 miles east.

Chuck and I searched and located some land where we wanted to build a house. It was 47 acres with only 150 feet frontage in 1978. The area wasn't considered good farmland. Since it was mostly trees, brush, and a creek, the price was cheaper than other more desirable locations. It was just what we wanted. Chuck saw it as a remote area where we could live away from the public eye and also have a place to train and entertain Project Partner teams.

It turned out to be a wonderful place to build a house, his next major project. One adventure followed another. The Warren County Farm Bureau made various trees available to area farmers each year. Chuck discovered he could have about three hundred small pine trees, each about a foot tall. With the help of the Boy Scouts, all three hundred were planted. Chuck also wanted a barn, so he built it with his son Paul's help that same fall. With his tractor, which he had brought from Wichita, he felt like a farmer even though he didn't have time for true farming. The house and all the property were dedicated to the Lord's service during the Board of Directors meeting in October 1979.

A New Idea: A Missions Cruise

Another new idea came to Chuck, but then he always had a new idea to try out. In 1976, he got the idea for a missions cruise in the Caribbean. A Christian cruise would interest people who enjoyed this kind of travel, and he could show them what the Lord was doing on some of the islands where Project Partner had been working. He found Commodore Cruise line easy to work with and booked passage on it for our first cruise adventure.

In January 1977, Project Partner embarked on its first cruise in the Caribbean. For Chuck it was another new way to get people involved in missions, and it was highly successful. Dr. Eugene Sterner, speaker for the *Christian Brotherhood Hour*, a church of God program, came as guest speaker. The ports of Cap Haitian, Puerto Plata, San Juan, and St. Thomas were used for an introduction to missions.

The idea of taking Christians on a missions cruise worked so well we repeated it in 1978 and 1979, and then we got the idea to charter a whole ship. It was a huge undertaking because Chuck would have to sign a contract of over a half-million dollars. We laid out a plan as to how many people we would have to have signed up by the time the contract was to be signed. Enlisting the help of a well-known singer in those days, Doug Oldham, who was holding concerts all across the United States and had sung for four presidents as well as the Queen of England, was one of the reasons it was successful. Doug signed up people at his concerts. Chuck also enlisted a representative in several different states to recruit people. By the time the contract was signed, we had over two-thirds of the total passengers needed. When the ship sailed in January 1980, every room was filled.

When you charter a whole ship, you have control of all the activities. We chose the movies, closed the slot machines, closed the bar except for soft drinks, and selected all the entertainment. Chuck brought Dr. Dale Oldham, a renowned speaker of the *Christian Brotherhood Hour* as well as the father of Doug Oldham, as the speaker for the services each evening. Doug Oldham was a soloist. Sandi Patty was just starting out in her career, so she was enlisted to sing as well. Within a few years, she was added to the Gospel Music Hall of Fame and won thirty-nine Dove Awards, five Grammy Awards, and numerous other awards.

Once again Chuck chose the ports of call, this time Kingston, Jamaica; Port-au-Prince, Haiti; and Puerto Plata in the Dominican Republic. Our plan was to show our people the needs in these countries and how the Lord was working.

Jamaica had been a socialist country for several years and had just become a democracy. Our chartered ship was the first cruise ship back in Kingston Harbor. In honor of the event, Kingston provided a special welcome ceremony on the dock with the mayor and other city dignitaries. Adding to the big occasion, Doug Oldham gave two concerts at a big hotel. Both concerts were packed.

We made one big mistake. I made it first. We were docked in Kingston, Jamaica. Some of our Jamaican friends asked if they could go on board and see the ship. "Sure," I replied, "I'll show you around." They were intrigued with the cabins and berths. They loved the stairs and the lounges. The great entertainment hall made their eyes light up. They had never seen anything like our ship before.

Then I opened the door to the dining room. Immediately I knew I had made a mistake. The staff was preparing the food for the midnight buffet. Typical of most cruise ships, this midnight buffet was lavish. There were all kinds of food and everything one could think of, including fancy ice carvings. I tried to turn the group around, but they had caught a glimpse and scurried around me so fast I found myself at the back of the group. They wanted to see. Their eyes were big. They were leaning over the rail and just drinking in the beauty of all the trays and bowls of food. They were even taking big breaths to enjoy the smells as well as the sights.

These people were lucky to have three scant meals a day. They had just come from a socialistic society back into a democracy, and just getting food on the table had been a difficult task for a long time. Here we "rich Americans" had three great meals and then something this lavish at midnight. To them it was incomprehensible. I felt ashamed and embarrassed, first that so much food had been prepared for us, and then because they saw it and couldn't have any. This beautiful, lavish buffet was not for them. I would have given anything if they had not seen it, or better yet, if I could have invited them in to eat.

As I was finally getting them toward the door to leave, Chuck made the same mistake with another group who had asked for a tour. It was an unforgettable experience for them as well to see the enormous amount of food and for us to be so embarrassed about our affluence.

Port-au-Prince was the next stop. We had buses ready to take the people to visit schools, churches, and orphanages established by Rev. Joe Surin, a leading pastor Project Partner was working with. Haiti was the poorest country in the Western Hemisphere, and its desperate needs got into our people's hearts. They were getting a good taste of what life was like in other countries.

Last on the itinerary was Puerto Plata. There the people visited churches, schools, and clinics to see how the islanders lived. It was not as poor as Haiti but very different from our country.

The cruises were very successful. We arranged three more but did not book the whole ship for them. The idea was catching on with other Christian groups. Chuck was always looking for new things he wanted to try, so when he discovered others were taking this path, he decided the Lord would use him in other ways to fulfill his purpose of recruiting people to be a part of the Great Commission.

Monterrey Youth Experience

A new question entered Chuck's mind as to how he could get more young people to experience missions in Mexico. It was great taking individuals on teams but was there a better way? With this desire, he contacted Enrique Cepeda, by then a key pastor in Monterrey at the Castillo del Rey, and he and Chuck put together a program called the

Monterrey Youth Experience. With this program, youth from various churches across the U.S. could all come together at one time in June in Mexico. The news got out, the youth poured in, and it was a great adventure for all of them. The young people saw opportunities to serve the Lord in ways they had never conceived. It was new. It was serving. It was adventure and in another country. They liked it.

Charles Stanley, music professor at University of Texas at El Paso, volunteered to direct this event for several years in the mid-eighties. The youth groups led vacation Bible schools, painted and repaired churches, and served in all kinds of ways and areas around Monterrey. They stayed together at Castillo del Rey, since the church had dorms and dining facilities. This arrangement gave them the joy of teamwork for the Lord and enabled them to have services together. It was a very positive experience and impacted the Mexican children as well as the youth from the U.S. To this day, people still come to me and tell me about the impact those trips to Mexico had on their life. It was and is the thing to do to share the Lord with our neighbors.

Actually this Monterrey Youth Experience was the inspiration for many churches to develop programs to take their youth groups on mission trips, be it Appalachia or Mexico. It is exciting to see how the idea has caught the interest of Christian leaders and how it is continuing to impact thousands of young people today.

Agape Children's Ministry

Chuck had seen too many hungry, needy children to just walk on by. He knew in his heart he had to do something. With this purpose in mind, he contacted Compassion International and asked if he could come for a visit. Of course the staff at Compassion welcomed him. When he told them he wanted Project Partner to establish a child sponsorship program for children in Haiti, Guatemala, Nicaragua, Honduras, Costa Rica, Panama, and South America, the leaders pulled out their program and shared their methods and plans.

Chuck chose to call his program the Agape Children's Ministry because *agape* is the Greek word for "love." By January 1979, he had the staff for it and a leader for it in several countries. The Agape Children's Ministry was on its way.

The ministry was very successful and totally changed hundreds of children's lives during its twenty years of operation. The first Agape child in Costa Rica turned out to be a pastor in San Jose when he grew up. Other children were able to find their places into all different trades and professions as they matured. The most rewarding part was they knew the Lord and had become Christians. Later, Chuck took the Agape program into Asia where it was very productive in India and China.

But was there more? About this time a friend gave Chuck another challenge.

What would this be?

Chapter Sixteen
DISCOVERING ASIA

Ohio seemed like just the right place to be for Chuck's growing ministry. The pastors and churches from Dayton to Cincinnati all welcomed him. More people became excited about the idea of missions ministry when they heard him speak, people who had never conceived the idea they could personally make a difference in this world just by joining his team or by volunteering on his trips. They too were discovering the joy of sharing this new way of serving God by connecting with their brothers and sisters in other countries. The ministry continued to grow in this new location, and Chuck was blessed to see it.

By now you know what challenges did for Chuck Thomas. One day a missionary friend asked, "Chuck, why have you spent so much time and energy in Central and South America and neglected the rest of the world? What you are doing is great, but don't you know 65 percent of the world's people live in Asia alone? Most of those people have never even heard the name of Jesus."

That comment was all it took for Chuck to start praying about Asia and if he was to be involved in that part of the world. He went back to his basic question, why not? He had his answer, and he booked a flight for the summer of 1981 to Japan, Korea, Hong Kong, Thailand, Singapore, and the Philippines. Of course, this trip wouldn't be just for him alone. When the word got out we were going to take a team to Asia, the phone began ringing. Numerous people wanted to go.

Asia 1981

Since this first team to Asia was composed of people from cities across the U.S., Chuck planned for everyone to meet at Chicago's O'Hare airport before departure to Tokyo. Gathering the team in a corner of the terminal, Chuck used the time before boarding to do an orientation for this new adventure. Right up front he stated he wanted team members to see this new world not as tourists but through the eyes of Jesus Christ. He emphasized they were to be aware Jesus was walking beside them, and he would be looking at the same things they would be looking at. They were to consider how Jesus would see what they saw. What would Jesus be thinking, and what would Jesus be feeling for the people who would seem so foreign?

Chuck stressed his joy of being able to see that part of the world and the extraordinary fellowship with other Christians we would no doubt have, even though we didn't speak their language or have their customs or culture. On his list of orientation topics was the importance of being loving, patient, congenial, and soft-spoken; having soft laughter, a calm appearance, and a demeanor showing the joy of the Lord. Also, he told us to expect problems—problems in communication, scheduling, time plans, and unexpected differences in culture. He used the term "hang loose" to communicate how we were to respond to whatever happened.

The Lord was putting Asia in Chuck's heart. He too wanted to see this part of the world through the eyes of Jesus. Already his heart was aching for those millions who had no knowledge of who Jesus is.

Experiencing Japan, seeing the Shinto shrines, and being exposed to all the differences in culture were new and powerful for us and the team. It was very difficult to find a Christian church; however, we had made arrangements to meet up with some missionaries. One of them, Phil Kinley when he first came to Anderson College had worked for Chuck at the East Side Jersey Dairy Bar. It was a privilege to see what he had been able to do as a missionary since there had been no Christian influence in Japan until after WWII, and still Christian presence was minimal.

Korea was different. There we had the joy of being with many Christian believers. Korea had some powerful churches, including the largest church in the world led by Pastor Cho. The Presbyterian churches were huge too. The most interesting thing to Chuck was the morning prayer meetings. At 5 or 6 a.m. every day, multitudes of believers were at the churches and on their knees. These were Christians who put their life before the Lord in earnest.

Hong Kong was most interesting—a busy, busy place and a shopper's paradise, filled with people on those two bits of land. But where was the church? The citizens were living in the shadow of China and under the control of Chairman Mao's influence. Hong Kong was still a British colony and under British protection. Looking into the faces of those throngs on the street, Chuck voiced the wonder in his heart as to how many of them even knew about Jesus Christ.

The vast multitudes of unreached people in Asia touched Chuck's heart. As we boarded the flight to return home, he was talking about the places he hadn't seen and was concerned about their knowledge of Jesus. He wanted to see the extent the gospel had reached in mainland China and in Thailand, Singapore, and the Philippines. His eyes had seen and his heart had been touched. He was wondering how he was to respond.

Smuggling Bibles into China?

Chuck's next plan was to take a team into China, as the country had just opened its doors to visitors from the rest of the world. Before plans could be finalized, however, something came up requiring his attention, so he asked me to lead the team. We would be among the first foreigners to visit Peking (now called Beijing) and Shanghai.

It was easy to form that first group to go into China, since it would be a totally new adventure for even our most experienced team members. In October of 1982, with me as team leader, the group flew into Hong Kong to get our visas to visit China and catch our breath. Before we left Hong Kong to go to Beijing and Shanghai, a friend took us to visit Dr. Jonathan Chao, the president of the Chinese Research Center. He took the time to tell us what was going on in China.

In 1950, Mao Tse-tung, the communist dictator, had taken over China and forced all missionaries to leave. The Bamboo Curtain went down, shutting out any news for some thirty-plus years. When the missionaries left, there were fewer than a million Christians. We in the West didn't know if the church had died or if any Christians remained. We had heard the Cultural Revolution was bad, whatever that meant. Researchers were just beginning to get information from China and find out how the church had survived during those years of persecution and terror. Dr. Chao and his workers were monitoring radio broadcasts, newspapers, letters, and anything else they could get that would offer inside information.

The borders were still closed, and we were told that getting in and out of China was very difficult. But we were going in. We would be under the complete authority of the China Travel Agency all the time we were there, and the agency would dictate our schedule and plans for us. The agency would control everything we did.

I met with Dr. Chao alone for a few minutes, and he informed me of the great need for Bibles in China. He then asked me if I would take some into the country. My immediate thought was, "I didn't bargain for this. I'm not sure I can do it."

"There won't be any problem for you," he said. "It's not really illegal. If the authorities find the Bibles, they will simply take them away and return them to you when you return to Hong Kong. There shouldn't be any problem at all."

"Okay, if it's no big deal, I'll try it. How many are you talking about?" I asked.

"I have a hundred here ready for you to take. They are small and black with no printing on the outside, so they won't be recognized," he replied.

He showed them to me. Well, I didn't recognize them as Bibles, and since they were printed in Chinese, I couldn't even figure out if I was holding them right side up or upside down.

"Here is the man's name to give them to," Dr. Chao explained. "It's Mr. Pei. And on this other piece of paper is his phone number. You might want to put this information in different places in your purse in case someone goes through your purse." He spoke rather softly as he said this last comment.

According to Dr. Chao, Bibles were rare in China because in the 1960s they were all confiscated and burned. The communist leaders had closed the churches and used the buildings for storage or turned them into communist headquarters. Most pastors were put in prison. Chinese Christians were very anxious to get Bibles.

I hadn't bargained to do such a thing, but by this point I felt I was already committed and didn't want to back out. After all, they were Bibles, and I did want the Chinese to have Bibles, didn't I?

"Don't use the word 'Bible'," Dr. Chao continued. "Instead, use the word 'gift.' Your room will probably be bugged."

This adventure was getting more complicated all the time. Maybe Dr. Chao thought I was the kind of person who liked to do this sort of thing. He told me when I arrived in to Shanghai to call Mr. Pei, and he would meet me and take the Bibles. I asked him if this handoff was all there was to it, and he assured me, "Yes, it will be simple." That was all the instruction I received.

The first thing I did was to call Chuck and ask him about this new development. Phone calls from Hong Kong to the United States were not easy in those days, but I managed to make the connection. "What should I do, Chuck? This sounds scary."

Chuck, the master encourager, said, "Honey, go for it. Why not? The Lord will go with you. This is just the opportunity to help get the gospel to the Chinese, and I will be specifically praying for you all the time." His only regret was he couldn't go with us.

Having done nothing like this before, the team members and I took the Bibles to our hotel, put them in the middle of the floor of my room, and prayed over them. "Lord, let us get these Bibles into China." Then we wrapped them with our clothes, hiding them in our suitcases as well as we knew how, and headed for the airport.

Our first stop was Beijing, and I was nervous. We went through immigration easily and headed on to pick up our bags and go through customs. We waited and waited for those bags. The conveyor belt just kept going round and round with nothing on it. The more I watched it, the more anxious I became. I was sitting there chewing my fingernails. Were the officials going to find the Bibles? Was I going to get in trouble? "Okay, Lord, help me do this," I prayed. "Please help me. I can't imagine what they will do to me if they catch me with these Bibles. What have I gotten myself into?"

For an hour we waited, and finally the bags appeared on the conveyer. I'd had plenty of time to pray and chew my fingernails. We grabbed them and headed for customs. When we got there, the official asked me if we were a group. When I told him we were, he just motioned for us to go on through. No problem at all. Just like Dr. Chao had said.

We spent a few days in Beijing, and then we flew on to Shanghai on Sunday afternoon. The hotel there was a little better than Beijing, but not much. The front doors to all hotels were sealed shut in those days so no one could use them. We had to use the side entrance. There was a long drive to the side entrance and a big fence around everything. No Chinese were allowed in the hotel except staff. The hotel was only for foreigners.

I went to my room to make the call to Mr. Pei, but first I had to figure out how to use the telephone. Telephones looked basically the same in every country, but the telephone system was always different. How was I to do this? I sure couldn't ask for help. That would be a good way to get in trouble. I experimented a bit and managed to get a phone line out of the hotel. I dialed the number, the phone rang, and a woman answered in Chinese. Somehow I didn't expect this. After all, doing something like I was doing was so totally new to me.

"Is Mr. Pei there?" I stammered. She said something I could not understand, and then the phone was silent. I didn't know if she said, "Lady, you have the wrong number," or if she had left the phone to get him.

After what seemed an extensive wait, Mr. Pei answered in English. What a relief! "Mr. Pei," I said, "I am Donna Thomas from America. I have a small group here with me. We were just in Hong Kong and met some great people there. They asked me to give you their greetings. Also, we have brought some gifts for you."

"Oh, fine," he replied.

"Where can I meet you and give you these gifts?" I asked.

"What is your schedule for tomorrow?" he asked.

"Well, we'll be going to a commune (a community of people assigned to live and work together for the government) in the morning, and then the guide said we'd be at a botanical garden in the afternoon," I replied. "Oh yes, we will be at the Number One Department Store tomorrow at 5 p.m. Would that work out all right as a place to meet you?"

"It will be fine. Where should I meet you?" he responded.

I was caught off guard once again. I hadn't figured this adventure all out yet. Let's see, what would be in a department store in China? Every department store I had ever been in had a shoe department. Surely there would be one in a China department store too. Yes, the shoe department would probably be a good place to meet. "How about in the shoe department?" I offered.

"That will be fine," he replied. Then another question. "How will I know you?"

I thought he could probably tell who I was since I looked like a typical American, but I didn't say that. "Well, I'll have on a yellow blouse and a blue skirt," was my answer.

The next morning as our group met for breakfast, I discovered we had a different guide who was very pro-government. He had been taught to think "the end justifies the means." Whatever it took to have communism for the whole world was worth it, even if it meant killing people. I knew I didn't have a friend in him, and he surely didn't need to know what we were doing.

Our group boarded the bus early. It was October, so we could use our coats to cover the bundles of Bibles. We sat in the back of the bus and let the eight people the government had added to our group sit in the front. Hopefully the guide would not know what was going on. What would we do if he found out?

Our first stop was the commune. There were 18,000 people living there, all under government control. They worked for a common cause. It didn't matter if a person was lazy or worked hard. All got the same pay. As you might guess, there weren't very many hard workers.

We went first to the headquarters of the commune, where the leaders sat us down around a table for tea. They brought each one a typical

Chinese cup with lid filled with sweet smelling Jasmine tea. As we sipped the tea, they shared the glories of communism and how great it was living in a commune. Then they took us to a kindergarten. The children were waiting for us and had a special program all prepared. Next was their hospital, which in my estimation left a hundred thousand things to be desired. But we did see acupuncture being practiced, and it was certainly different. Then, before lunch, we stopped at a factory and made a tour of their premises. There were lots of workers, but there weren't any working very hard. The whole factory seemed in slow motion.

Lunch was unbelievable. We were served twenty-seven courses. After the first ten, I stopped eating. When I asked what happened to the leftovers, I was told there was plenty of food, and leftovers were simply thrown away. I had trouble believing this response, because our guide had already showed us some homes. He had taken us through a display house, which had a small but adequate living space, a small bedroom, and a wee little kitchen in the back. The bed had a board for the mattress, and the kitchen had a wood burning stove and a bucket to carry in water. There was a television in the "typical" house; however, there were no electric outlets in any of the rooms or any electric lights. Obviously the television was there just for show. We were supposed to appreciate the great accommodations the government provided for the people. It was the People's Republic of China, after all.

When we were back on the bus, our guide told us he had good news for us. He had been able to rearrange our schedule, and he was excited to add some programs. We were going to see the Children's Palace that afternoon. A special program was planned just for us; therefore, he would speed up all the previously scheduled afternoon activities.

I hadn't planned for something like this. I questioned him on how the schedule was going to be changed and at what time we were going to be at the department store. He said we would be moving everything up so we would be at the department store at 3 p.m. instead of 5 p.m. "Oh my," I thought. "We will be there and gone before Mr. Pei comes." My heart sank. "How do I handle this? How is the Lord going to make our appointment work?"

The next stop was the Botanical Gardens. We filed off the bus and followed our guide down the path between the plants. I didn't go far because I was asking the Lord, "What am I supposed to do now? There's no phone here to call Mr. Pei. I don't know how to handle this situation."

Turning around, I went back to the bus, climbed on board, and sat down halfway back. I needed to pray and think. Then I noticed the bus driver was studying a little book of English. Maybe he could help me. Going up to him, I held my right hand to my mouth and ear like a telephone and said, "Hello, hello."

He knew what I wanted. Jumping out of his driver's seat, he motioned for me to follow him. We went down a different path, back through some trees to a little cabin. Inside there was a telephone. Great! Once again I had to figure out how to use this one.

I got it to work the first time, it rang, and the same lady at Mr. Pei's place answered in Chinese. When I asked again for Mr. Pei, the phone went silent. I felt more comfortable waiting this time, and shortly he answered. I told him of the schedule changes. He told me it would be no problem and he would be there at the new time. "Wow! Thank you, Lord." This delivering Bibles was getting to be a bit more than I had bargained for. It was supposed to be simple.

When we all got back on the bus, I told my group of the change in plans and assured them it was going to work out. They were to follow me into the store, and I would give Mr. Pei the Bibles I had first. Then they would come up one at a time and give him the Bibles they had.

At the Number One Department Store, I asked Peter, one of our team, if he would keep the guide occupied. I sure didn't want our guide to know what we were doing. He said he would take the guide to the electronics department. The rest of us would head quickly for the stairs to go down to the second floor and the shoe department.

The plan was working so far. Finding a pillar to stand by in the shoe department, I stopped there, looking very American in my yellow blouse and blue skirt. Soon a nice looking older Chinese man came over and introduced himself as Mr. Pei. He seemed a bit nervous, but I gave him the Bibles I had. Then one of our group came up and handed him a sack of Bibles, then another, and then I realized we had a new problem. The amount of Bibles eight people had brought in could not be carried out by one person. Too big a load. I hadn't thought of that.

"Mr. Pei, how can we get the rest of these gifts to you?" I asked.

"Where are you staying?" he asked. I really didn't know the name of the hotel so I showed him my key with the hotel name on it.

"Call me when you get back and I will meet you nearby" was his reply. He took the Bibles he was able to carry and quickly disappeared.

Finally back at the hotel, I headed for the phone for the third time and called Mr. Pei. He directed me to meet him out on the street, a bit farther up than the hotel, with the "gifts" at eight o'clock.

At that time of day in Shanghai, it was dark, very dark. The leaves of the many poplar trees were dancing in the wind. There were no street lights, and drivers mostly maneuvered without their headlights, flipping them on only when they thought there was something out there. The sound of the trucks and bicycles going by in the dark was eerie. I have a little "chicken" in my blood and didn't want to go out on the street alone. I enlisted the services of Homer Firestone, one of our group who had previously been a missionary to Bolivia. He met me at the door at eight o'clock. We walked out the side door, past the guard house where the guards said, "Good evening" to us in what seemed to be their newly acquired English, and on through the gate to the road outside.

On down the road a bit farther we stopped, waiting there in the shadows. Some trucks and bicycles went by in the dark. Only one flipped its lights at us. The dancing leaves on the poplars made the shadows eerie. It wasn't long before a bicycle came up to us. It was Mr. Pei.

This short Chinese man who spoke excellent English got off his bicycle and came closer. I realized at once this location was much better than the department store. Here we would have a chance to talk. I asked him what he was doing in Shanghai. He told me his purpose was to get "the bread" to his people. They so needed "the bread of life," and there were no resources to get it for them. He also told me his efforts to obtain Bibles were very dangerous for him. He had already been in prison three times, and he might go to prison again. "But," he added with conviction, "I have got to get the bread to our people, and this is why I am taking these Bibles." He was very nervous and did not tell me much more. He was anxious to be on his way. We had a short prayer together and then he left, speeding away on his bicycle in the dark. I knew I had just met a saint.

Chuck was waiting for us at the airport anxious to hear about all the experiences. When he heard about Mr. Pei, he said, "We've got to go again next year and take him some more Bibles. A man with that dedication needs all the help he can get. Imagine the risk this man takes so others, people he probably will never know, will hear about our Savior."

A New Program, Training National Pastors

On a previous trip to Peru, Chuck and I discovered many pastors had never received any training. None. Zero. They hadn't been to a

Bible school or seminary. They had only one Bible and no supportive materials. We asked if they had a concordance. They didn't know what that was. How about a Bible dictionary? No, and had never seen one. Maybe a book on preaching or speaking? Not one of those either. Okay, what could we do? With Chuck's encouragement, I started the program of training national pastors.

Our Mexican friend Enrique Cepeda had come under our umbrella at Project Partner back in 1982. We had been helping him, encouraging him, and working with him since that first bus trip to Mexico in 1962. He could be a great help with a pastors conference in Peru. I began planning this conference, knowing he would make an excellent interpreter.

Two excellent pastors/preachers agreed to go with me in the spring of 1983, and we spent a week teaching those Peruvian pastors. Rev. Billy Ball and Rev. David Grubbs were ready for that challenge. I also asked Enrique Cepeda to go as our interpreter. Yes, he was ready for that challenge.

With research I found Erdman's Commentaries in Spanish along with a Bible dictionary. Next was to raise the funds to provide these resources for all and to fund the trip and conference expenses. People who believed in Project Partner rose to the occasion, and that spring we held the first National Pastors Training Conference in Lima, Peru, to around ninety native pastors. What a joy it was to see their response. They had never been to anything like this training and would have sat on those wooden benches for twenty consecutive hours just to hear and absorb what more they could learn to help their people. At the final service, each one came forward to receive a Certificate of Accomplishment. Can you imagine the smiles on their faces as they accepted it?

I personally was blessed so much by this opportunity of expanding their ministry and outreach. Obviously this was no time to quit but to move forward, so I scheduled another national pastors training conference for the spring of 1984. I took Dewayne Repass, Henry Skaggs, and Bob Preston. That time even more Peruvian pastors came. We could feel their excitement and anticipation. One of the young pastors from the Amazon area was scanning the printed program when he came to me and said, "I see we have a session on the leadership of the Holy Spirit. I am so glad. I have heard there is a Holy Spirit, but I don't know anything about him and I want to know."

The next day Henry Skaggs preached a great message on the Holy Spirit. When he finished, the pastors began to call out with loud voices,

"Please don't stop preaching. We want to hear more about the Holy Spirit." Henry did continue teaching for another thirty minutes or so.

Another outstanding part of that week was the miracle of tongues. Missionary Paul Butz was translating for Dewayne Repass. In the middle of the message, Paul stopped translating and told us the pastors were understanding Dewayne without him. He took a seat on the front row while Dewayne continued his message. That was the only session like that, but it certainly stood out.

Then there was the miracle of the watches. Dewayne had been able to obtain around one hundred wristwatches to take as a gift to the pastors. He was excited that each of the pastors would have one; however, he wasn't aware of the problem of taking them through customs. When the customs people opened Dewayne's briefcase and saw so many watches, one of the officials immediately placed a machine gun on Dewayne's chest and yelled, "Contra!" It took the grace of the Lord and some fast praying for the man to lower the gun and allow us to take the watches on into Peru. The last session of the conference concluded with Dewayne handing each pastor a wristwatch and the other speakers presenting the pastors with a Certificate of Ministry.

At yet another conference held later, a pastor named Narciso Zamora was telling of his vision to go to Ecuador and plant churches. Immediately the room was filled with a buzz of excitement, and Narciso went to the altar to ask for prayer. The pastors then chose to take an offering for him. It was over $300 U.S. dollars. After the service, our team confessed that together we had only contributed $90. Those Peruvian pastors had sacrificed greatly to encourage their fellow pastor to go. Narciso planted more than five congregations before officials forced him to leave the country. He then went to Chile to continue his church-planting ministry. Later he wrote a book, *Walking Man,* telling his story of walking with the Lord.

With these responses, I could see that this method of training national pastors could have tremendous consequences for the kingdom of God. The pastors trained would be reaching and teaching all across their country and doing things a missionary could never accomplish. Yes, empowering pastors in other countries was a worthy effort, and Latin America was ready.

I found other American pastors wanting to serve in this way, and we held conferences in Argentina, Columbia, Brazil, Ecuador, Panama, Costa Rica, Nicaragua, Honduras, Guatemala, Mexico, Haiti, Dominican Republic, and Jamaica.

These training conferences were so well received and seemed such a tremendous help. After the trips Chuck and I had recently taken to Asia, I could see the pastors there would benefit from them too. After all, the Lord did say to go to all the world and take the gospel. We were ready.

World Trip 1983

In 1983 Chuck planned an extensive trip around the world to visit ministry partners and meet new ones. Twelve brave souls joined us in Los Angeles before we headed on to Japan and then into Shanghai and Beijing for another unforgettable China experience. Chuck had put the opportunity to take Bibles to Mr. Pei in the itinerary in Shanghai. It was exciting for Chuck to meet Mr. Pei and have the privilege of delivering Bibles to him. This brave man was later put in prison again and was sentenced to be executed. When Chuck heard about his circumstances, he contacted the U.S. State Department and, working with his congressmen, was able to help Mr. Pei be released.

Next on our trip was Hong Kong; Bangkok and up country in Thailand; on to New Delhi and Bombay, India; and then we headed to Nairobi, Kenya, for the World Conference of the Church of God. Leaving there, we visited churches in Cairo, made a brief stop in Lebanon, and then explored Rome and all its history before our return to home base.

Bad News

It was a phenomenal trip; however, Chuck wasn't feeling well on most of it. When he was home, he went to his doctor for a checkup. He was feeling extreme fatigue and lack of energy. He also seemed to have a pain in his chest at times, which he called a "spell." His doctor put him through various texts and examinations, and then he told Chuck he had a heart problem. Chuck had a friend in Wichita who was a heart specialist, so we flew there to get his opinion. That doctor confirmed there was a problem with Chuck's heart and suggested he go to the famed Mayo Clinic in Rochester, Minnesota. At Mayo he was told he had cardiomyopathy (a condition in which the heart muscles deteriorate and enlarge; they can't pump effectively, and it's just a matter of time before death). The experts at Mayo said there was nothing they could do for him.

It wasn't long before Chuck's condition worsened and he couldn't keep up the pace. With great reluctance, he turned in his resignation as president of Project Partner in November 1983. This news sent the board of directors searching for several months for his replacement. Chuck continued to deteriorate physically, his pace slowed, his color faded, his energy was gone, and yet the Lord wasn't finished with him.

In February of 1984, the chairman of the board came into my office to tell me the board had decided they would like me to take the position of president, as I was cofounder and well acquainted with the entire ministry. My reaction was like Moses'—surely not me. I immediately went to Chuck to get his wisdom, and as Mr. Encourager, he was quick to tell me I could do it and he would support me. He was one who was always encouraging others to step forward for the Lord in whatever position appeared. With his endorsement and lots of prayer, I accepted the position.

Life was different for Chuck from that point on. He was still always thinking of new ideas and ways to expand the ministry, but he had to bury those ideas in his prayers, as he was not able to fulfill them. His physical stamina kept him from functioning the way he wanted. He was, however, more than willing to help me in my new role in every way he could. When I would be searching for a solution to a problem or opportunity, I would immediately go to him for his advice and counsel. He did find ways to serve at church and in various small activities at Project Partner, but the old Chuck Thomas wasn't functioning any longer. He was on the sidelines. What was going to happen to him?

Chapter Seventeen
NEW DIRECTIONS

"What's this? A new president? But she's not new." Those were a few of the sentiments circulating around the Project Partner office when I was introduced to the staff as the new president. Chuck had been gone for four months, and they were expecting someone new to step into his shoes.

Their thoughts echoed mine, except my first commitment was to serve the Lord. I knew what was happening to Chuck and Project Partner was the Lord's plan, not mine. "Okay, Father. You're the boss," I prayed. "I want your input, direction, and guidance every morning. I can't do this alone. This job is bigger than I am, so if you want it to go forward, tell me what to do."

Pastor Training in Asia

Soon I had a team of three pastors ready to go to Asia. We flew off to the Philippines to do a week's training for around seventy-five pastors there. That conference was as productive as the ones we had done in Peru. Yes, God had his plans for Project Partner in this part of the world as well.

Since the team had never been to Asia before, I also included a visit to Hong Kong. We were just going to see the city, the sights, and visit a friend, Arthur Gee. Arthur was on the staff of what is now known as Partners International. During our meeting with Arthur, he told me he had a Chinese pastor he wanted me to meet who lived in Macau, the small Portuguese province on the edge of China and just west of Hong Kong. No problem. Chuck had taught me to enjoy adventure, and I was ready to go.

Arthur led me to the jetfoil, which took us on the short trip across the sea to Macau. After exiting immigration, he introduced me to a tall Chinese man waiting for us at the pier. We climbed into his car, and he took us to his church in the center of the business district. We took a brief look at his sanctuary and went to his office, where he seated us and gave us tea, of course. As the pastor spread a blueprint before me, Arthur translated, "He wants you to see this blueprint of a church he has permission to build in mainland China."

"This is really unheard of, and it is amazing he has it," Arthur commented. "The Chinese government has been destroying churches, not allowing new ones to be built. Really, Donna, since it has only been a very few years since the doors of China have opened, this is certainly a tremendous miracle. Here it is 1984, and the first foreigners were allowed to come to China just before 1980. As you know, Mao and his Cultural Revolution did away with religions, with Christianity, with Bibles, and burned churches or turned them into communist headquarters or cattle barns. No one was allowed to be a Christian, and here we are just a few years later. Mao is dead, but the same communist system is still in place."

"Arthur, you are telling me that he can build a church in mainland China; he actually has permission to build a church building?" I said.

"Yes, the pastor has the permission, but he needs the funds to build it. He is asking now if you can find the money for it."

"How much will it take? I have only been president of Project Partner for a month, and there isn't any money at all for something like this."

"He is asking for $12,000. That really isn't too much for this big a building, but I understand your problem. Do you think you can find this kind of money?"

Twelve thousand dollars. I was new at this job, and I had no idea where I could find that much money. We finished our tea, and Arthur and I climbed back into the pastor's car for a tour of Macau. Even though the perimeters were only a little more than a mile square, he wanted us to see all the interesting places.

I wrestled with the problem (or opportunity) as the pastor drove us around. Was it something the Lord would have Project Partner do? How would I ever be able to find that much money? I couldn't do it, but I knew it must happen. Just before Arthur and I caught the jetfoil back to Hong Kong, I told the pastor if he would give me a year, I would find the funds for him.

As we boarded the flight for the trip home the next morning, I ask my three pastor friends to get their churches to help. They too were excited about it and joined in prayer, knowing this was an impossible project except with the blessing of the Lord.

Helping to Build a Church in Mainland China

Returning home, I discovered it wasn't difficult to raise the funds needed. I contacted several churches, and amazingly each one said yes, they would love to help the Chinese people learn about Christ. It happened. A new church building was actually built in mainland China in 1984, and by faith and trust I had a part in it. God does the impossible. So in March of 1985, I was back in Macau for the dedication of what was probably the first new church building in China after Mao's Cultural Revolution.

It was wonderful to dedicate that church building. I could hardly imagine that through Project Partner, I'd had the privilege of helping this pastor build this exceptional church building. It was hard to believe it was really happening, and our ministry had a part in it. The dedication service was basically for the workers, and I also had the privilege of telling them who Jesus is and what he could do for them.

After that wonderful afternoon dedicating the building, the pastor came to me and said, "I need to tell you more about this building. It is actually the headquarters of the underground church."

"What? You mean this building already has this kind of ministry?"

"Oh yes, we have 350 pastors and 200,000 believers," he replied.

I was totally amazed. Obviously I continued to work with him. He'd helped put new direction into the ministry of Project Partner.

Opening the Door to India

That October a young man from India named Samuel Stephens came to the office. He had been sent to the United States by his father to find some money for their ministry. It was quite an assignment, and he was depending on the Lord to get him in the right places. He showed me pictures of their work in villages across India, adding most interesting stories. Of course, he needed money. He asked for $4,000 to build a church in one of those villages. Again I didn't have the funds and also didn't know this young man who had suddenly just appeared. No, I couldn't do that, I informed him. Then he showed me pictures of children that needed support. Well, yes, we had our Agape child support program.

"Samuel," I said, "If you can get me a letter of recommendation from the president of the Evangelical Fellowship of Asia and one from the president of the Evangelical Fellowship of India, I will help you with your children's program."

Samuel didn't know those leaders, but before long he had their recommendation in my hands. I had to start helping him with his children's program. A bit later he called from the West Coast, and the Lord encouraged me to provide the funds for him to come to see me again. I was impressed with what he showed me and asked him to show his pictures at staff meeting that day. Before he was finished, I knew the Lord wanted us to work more extensively with him. It was the beginning of another delightful and productive relationship with a national Christian leader, Samuel Stephens, and the India Gospel League.

A Wider Vision

The vision for the future was getting clearer. I turned the short-term mission trips over to one of the Project Partner staff who wanted to continue this ministry, and my focus turned a new direction, into developing partnerships with productive national leaders in their own country. The advantages were that they had always lived there, they knew the language, they didn't need a visa or passport to travel there, they were a part of the culture, they enjoyed their kind of food, they already had a very productive ministry, and they had a heart to reach the lost across their own country. The church in the West at that time was only sending missionaries, not partnering with productive national leaders. It was new. It wasn't being done. But it was how the Lord was directing us. My eyes were open to new possibilities.

Besides Enrique Cepeda from Mexico, the pastor in China, and Samuel Stephens in India, Chuck and I knew many other national leaders with whom we could establish partnerships. They included Ali Velasquez, a church planter in Nicaragua; Guillermo Villanueva, an evangelist in Mexico; Lener Cauper, a pastor and leader in Peru; Andrey Bondarenko, an evangelist in Russia and Latvia; Peter Dugulescu, a leader and director in Romania; and Joe Surin, a church planter in Haiti. As I contacted them and each one made the commitment to become a "partner" with us, I enlisted churches across the U.S. to be a part of their team. These churches put them in their mission budget, but even more than that, they sent teams to help. Their pastors went with me for pastor training conferences; they wanted the national leaders for their mission conferences, and precious relationships were formed. These partnerships were an example of the unity of those serving the Lord as his disciples here at this time. It was a special unity across the lines of race, language, and culture as all were focused on making disciples of all nations.

The teams I would be enlisting in the future would be to train pastors in these countries, to serve their people medically, and to catch the vision of what wonderful things the Lord was accomplishing with these productive national leaders.

More Pastor Training Conferences

As the Lord led us further into Asia and the Middle East, we held more pastor training conferences in India, Egypt, the Philippines, and China. The ones in China were with the endorsement of the Religious Affairs Director of the Communist Party.

The first one in Egypt was interesting. There I was bringing two American pastors with me at the invitation of the Egyptian church. It wasn't until I arrived with the team that they realized I was a woman. They didn't work with women, period, so it was an awkward situation for them. They finally decided to let me proceed, as I had the funding for the conference. It all turned out well, so well in fact that they invited me back several times for future conferences.

If we could count the number of pastors trained through this program alone, it would be astounding. Hundreds of thousands for sure. If we could fully realize the impact of their ministries, we would all be praising the Lord. This ministry is still going strong with numerous American pastors accepting the challenge. Yes, training native pastors and leaders is the way to go. It produces for the Lord in ways we can never imagine.

God Changes Circumstances Again

Three years later in March, as I left on a mission trip to train pastors in Haiti with Joe Surin, Chuck was at home struggling with his loss of ability to be active for the Lord. He had lost weight, was continually tired and weak, and actually looked quite gray. God had something more for him, and it was time. Here was the answer to our prayers. Here is his story as he wrote it.

HE TOUCHED ME!
By Charles F. Thomas
(June 1987 edition of Project Partner's newsletter, "Onward")

I have been miraculously, instantaneously, totally and completely healed. It happened on March 14, 1987, at 3 p.m.

For more than ten years I have suffered from a heart problem. For the last four years I have been on total disability. I had to resign as President of Project Partner With Christ, and my ministry was limited to what I could do as a volunteer in the local church.

I suffered a lot of pain, shortness of breath, and I had to be very careful of what I did because the slightest amount of exertion would just wipe me out. My situation was somewhat complex because I had some cardiomyopathy, some vascular restriction and a left bundle branch block; any one of the three was severe enough to cause me all the trouble I was experiencing, but the three together were devastating and debilitating. There did not seem much the cardiologists could do to help me.

Then it happened. On Sunday night March 8, I was feeling very badly. My family doctor was at church and when I told him how bad I was feeling and I was going back to the cardiologist for more testing. He said, "I'll be remembering you!" He was very encouraging to me for he was one more of the 100s of people who had assured me of their prayers. On Wednesday night, March 11 at prayer meeting, our pastor's wife, Jan Robold asked me, "Chuck, how are you feeling?" "Oh, just so-so," I replied. I didn't want to complain all the time but I felt pretty bad. Later she said the reason she had asked was because I didn't look good in the face. "I feel we need to put forth a concerted effort of prayer for you," she said. I thanked her and knew I really needed a touch of the Lord because I felt I was getting worse.

On Saturday, March 14 at 2 p.m., I was in the backyard of our home. Donna was in Haiti leading a Pastors Training Conference. I had a severe attack. The pain was very severe. I came into the living room of our home and slouched down on the couch. "Relax," I told myself. "Relax." I laid there and rested. At 3 o'clock, I looked at my watch and remembered I had been invited to dinner. I thought to myself, "I should take my shower soon so I can rest before I shave, and then rest again before I dress if I am going to make it for the 5:30 dinner."

I got up from the couch; the pain was gone. I breathed deeply to discover it really was gone. My thought was I should shower quickly before the pain returned. I didn't know I had been healed. I only knew the pain was gone and I felt great. I didn't tell anyone, but several people told me I looked good. I said, "I feel good, too." The next evening (Sunday), the first person I confided in was my doctor. I saw him at church and said, "Doctor, I think I have been healed." With a look of compassion and understanding he said, "Good, can you pinpoint the time?" I knew it was sometime between 2 and 3 o'clock the day before, so this was what I told him. The next few days were tremendous. I had excessive energy and stamina like I had not had for years. I did major repair work around the house, which had been seriously neglected as I had been unable to do it.

Donna returned on Friday at the Cincinnati airport. I met her. There was construction taking place, and the temporary gate was on the ramp level, which made it necessary to go down a long flight of stairs to the gate. After greeting her, I took her handbag. She took a good look at me and said, "You look good, Chuck." I said, "I feel good." She started up the stairs slowly, which was customary for me, but then she increased her pace to keep up with me. I reached the top of the stairs just a little ahead of her and she said, "What's with you?" She was amazed at how I managed the long staircase. "I will tell you later," I replied.

At the baggage carrousel, I took her bags, which I had not been able to do before and carried them to our car. As we climbed in the car I told her, "Donna, I think I've been healed." I related the past few days to her. "Wow, Praise the Lord! Our amazing Lord!" was her response.

When I shared the good news with our Pastor Claude Robold, he encouraged me to claim healing and proclaim it to all who I met. I explained to him, not only because my name is Thomas ("doubter"), I did not want to claim healing and then later get sick again and bring reproach to God. I was expecting some kind of a sign or witness of the Spirit affirming I was healed, but I did not know how it happened. It was sometime between 2 and 3 o'clock on Saturday afternoon, March 14. After more counsel and prayer, I told our pastor, "If I should die of a heart attack tomorrow, I want the record to show I have had two and one half weeks of complete healing."

My experience reminds me of the story in Matthew where a man was blind and Jesus healed him. The Pharisees began to question his parents and then the man himself. "How did this happen?" they asked him. He finally responded, "This one thing I know, once I was blind and now I see."

I know how he felt. People are very inquisitive and some doubt my story. But this one thing I know, "I suffered for years and had a lot of pain and misery, and now I don't."

My cardiologist's evaluation at this point is, "I don't think it is advisable and desirable to put you through all the tests necessary to validate medically your story. You feel good, enjoy it, and come back to see me in six months."

I can't get my pilot's medical certificate back without the test, so I can't fly as a pilot in command, but this is a minor limitation compared to all the joy I have in enjoying a tremendous amount of energy and vigorous stamina. My body is strong, and on the date of this writing (May 25, 1987), I have enjoyed two months and eleven days without a single pain or symptom of heart problem. How did it happen? He touched me and made me whole. Praise the Lord!

(This article appeared in the June 1987 edition of "Onward," the newsletter of Project Partner With Christ. Chuck wanted the opportunity to share with his friends the healing touch of God in his life. His family and co-workers at Project Partner can clearly see the blessing in the additional five years of life so graciously given to Chuck by our Lord. All of the things he accomplished during this time to assist Donna in leading Project Partner and insuring the well-being of the organization, as well as creating even deeper relationships with his family, were very important. Dan Harman, editor.)

A note about the last paragraph of Chuck's story:

Chuck kept a daily record of his recovery, counting the days, going from 25, then 50, and on to 100—and then he stopped counting. He certainly had been healed by Almighty God. Chuck did take a new examination with the FAA to regain his pilot's license. He was examined, tested, and quizzed. The FAA doctors and examiners turned him every way but loose and finally gave him a clean bill of health. He took the required test, yet in the typical process of governmental red tape, after eight months, he still didn't have his license. At last it came in the mail. Clutching the paper in his hand, Chuck yelled with a big grin, "I can fly again!" It was a joyful yell of praise to God. Chuck never had the desire to fly groups after receiving his license, but being given his "wings" back was just another confirmation of what God had done in his life.

Chuck's Next Challenge

Can you almost hear Chuck say, "Okay, Lord, what do you want me to do now?"

I offered him the position of president of Project Partner again, but his answer was it wasn't what he was supposed to do now. When a request from our partner in China came asking for a medical team to teach doctors in a hospital, however, he jumped at the chance. Yes, he could do that and he would love to do it. Chuck loved medicine and remembered well his days on the front lines during WWII. A new challenge and the health to tackle it. Chuck could see all kinds of possibilities ahead. He was ready to go. Of course. Why not?

A National Leaders Congress

With Chuck focusing on his next adventure, my attention turned back to the new vision the Lord had revealed for Project Partner's future. The next direction from the Lord was to bring all of the national leaders we'd been working with, together with their wives, to the States for a week. They could be encouraged and learn from each other. I called this event a congress. It was a great step of faith as I counted the cost of all those airline tickets, a week at a retreat center, and the logistics of getting the national leaders into churches to speak while they were here in the States. I had it scheduled for October 1989, but in January I began wondering if it really was going to happen. I didn't have one dime of the funds needed to pull it off.

One morning as I was starting my time with the Lord, I got this message: "Trust me." Where did that come from? I didn't know. I didn't hear a voice, but there it was in my heart and mind. With that assurance, I chose to proceed. By the first of September, every dollar that was needed was there. The Lord provided, and he provided ahead of time.

What a wonderful week it was. There was Enrique Cepeda and his wife, Lydia, from Mexico; Lener Cauper and his wife, Herma, from Peru; Joe Surin and his wife, Josie, from Haiti; Pastor Lam and his wife, ChiLing, from China; Samuel Stephens and his wife, Prati, from India; and Guillermo Villanueva and his wife, Betty, from Mexico. They were eager to learn from each other, and most of our time was spent with the agenda they formed among themselves. On the final day, I brought in Bishop Milton Grannum and Rev. Claude Robold to inspire and encourage them. What a precious prayer time we had before they were sent off, back to their countries to reach their multitudes for Christ.

Chuck's life and mine had changed directions dramatically since 1983 when he was diagnosed with a heart condition. God had been laying groundwork for what was about to happen in the next five years.

Chapter Eighteen
FIVE MORE YEARS

By June 1987, the old Chuck Thomas was back and anxious to start working again. A request had come to take a medical team to China, and it had stirred his blood. He was ready, wanting to get back into service for the Lord. On his previous trips to China, his heart had been broken. He'd seen how controlled everyone was by the government and how they were restricted from having churches or any religion, for that matter. He'd developed a deep longing to help the Chinese hear the gospel of Jesus Christ but had to put his desire aside when his heart problem was controlling him. Not any longer. The Lord had healed him, so he certainly wasn't finished with him yet. Chuck immediately started planning what he might do to take the gospel to China.

A Medical Ministry Begins

Chuck was soon off to Cincinnati to start recruiting a team of doctors from the universities and the hospitals in that vicinity. His idea was new for them, and several were ready to give it a try. He also started checking with area hospitals in both Cincinnati and Dayton as to their discarded medical equipment. He discovered an older but still functioning X-ray unit, which had just been replaced by a new one, was available. It would be a great asset in any part of the world. He also discovered there was a great deal of other, very usable medical equipment that was being replaced, and the hospitals were glad to donate it to Project Partner if it could be used to benefit people in other parts of the world.

Chuck's discovery of used medical equipment about to be discarded brought up a new challenge. He needed a warehouse to store these great gifts of medical equipment. Searching around, he was able to locate an abandoned warehouse in Middletown. It wasn't the best, but it would work. Then he found a truck that could haul the equipment there so he could store it until he found the right country and the right time to take it.

Chuck and Donna ready for China

It was the beginning of a medical ministry that would later be named Caring Partners. It was exactly the new role Chuck wanted at this time in his life. Yes, American teams and medical equipment could be sent to care for partners in Christ in other countries.

Chuck soon had the first medical team together. They would be going to Nicaragua. His contact there was with the AMEN churches and the Baptist Hospital. He had started working with them years earlier after the big earthquake in 1972. Assisting their clinics around Managua and helping and teaching in the hospital was fulfilling his desire to help the sick and the troubled in the name of the Lord. It was also developing the base for numerous medical personnel to see how they could be useful in foreign countries such as Nicaragua.

Medical Teams to China

China was next, and it was a bigger challenge. It was halfway around the world and such a different culture. Our Chinese pastor had made contact with the communist authorities in the city of Xingning (one million people), and they had asked for Chuck to bring a team to train their doctors and staff. Interesting. Just where was Xingning, and why did the communist authorities there want help? Searching a map of China, Chuck first found the province of Guongdong, just north of Hong Kong. And there was Xingning in the northeast section of Guongdong, a couple of hundred miles farther away. He was told the city had a hospital, but the workers there could certainly use some training and upgrading on their medical skills.

With Xingning as his focus, Chuck was able to get a shipping container and fill it with valuable medical equipment that would be useful in China. Making all the arrangements to ship it and get it through customs and into China was a mountain of a problem with tons of paperwork plus the bureaucracy, but he worked his way through it.

Recruiting twenty doctors in the Cincinnati area wasn't all that difficult, as this was new and exciting territory for Americans. Chuck gave them training as to the culture and arrangements they would encounter in China. As they gathered at the Cincinnati airport with their Project Partner jackets, their bags loaded with medicines and supplies, their families on hand for good-byes, their excitement was contagious. They were even excited those fourteen hours on their first leg of the journey to Hong Kong. Immigration and customs were no problem there, so off to the next flight to Guangzhou before the long bus ride to Xingning.

What a special reception was waiting for them in Xingning. It was more than they ever expected. They were the first Americans to come there to help the people, and being professionals and doctors, they were most welcome. The chairman of the United Front Religious Affairs Commission actually made arrangements for them to stay on the compound where the communist officials lived with their families. They were treated in the highest manner in Chinese culture. They had their meals together, making friends with these officials, and even went to the extent of teaching their children to sing "Jesus Loves Me" in their language. They were very well accepted and were asked to come back, making this trip the beginning of several trips to China, not only in the Guangdong Province but in several other provinces as well.

The team members spent their time giving lectures and teaching through demonstration. One thing they discovered was that every doctor smoked, not realizing the dangers of it. The American tobacco companies had been pushing cigarettes in Asia, as the market for them in the U.S. was declining. One brand was even named "Long Life." The container full of medical supplies actually arrived while the team was doing training. Chuck said it made a bigger impact with that kind of timing than if it had come before or after.

Besides helping these doctors and staff with their medical treatments, the more important blessing was yet to come. After Chuck and his team were gone, the officials asked our Chinese pastor what they could do for him. The Chinese officials wanted to do something for him in return for him providing the medical team and equipment. This request is a unique part of Chinese culture that at this point worked in a marvelous way for our Chinese pastor, for Chuck, and for the growth of the kingdom in that part of China. The pastor told them he would like to build a church in a certain area, and the authorities said that would be fine.

Soon Chuck took another team over, and on the agenda was the dedication of this church building. The Religious Affairs chairman started the dedication service by telling the congregation they were to listen to the Christians there, as it would make them better Chinese. Those words were so amazing to hear in 1989, in a communist country like China. The Lord had certainly enabled Chuck and his teams to do seemingly the impossible.

Those two team trips were just the beginning, and Chuck continued to work with the Chinese pastor as well. His teams that came next trained more doctors, helped in more hospitals, and facilitated the growth of the Chinese church as well as the building of many church buildings. Working together with our Chinese pastor friend, they were extending the kingdom of God in new territories that were and still are considered impossible.

Chuck's teams of doctors were excited to be part of his new medical ministry. It was great. They were doing the impossible, and it was working. They loved Chuck and greatly appreciated the opportunity to use their skills in helping change the world under the banner of Jesus Christ.

Teamwork: Chuck and Disney

The mother of one of Chuck's doctors lived in Orlando, Florida, and was working in the offices of Disney World. Of course, the doctor told his mother all about his trip and what a blessing it was to the Chinese and also what a blessing it was to him. That set his mother thinking. She realized that her supervisor had a problem, and maybe she had a solution. The supervisor had tons of Disney shirts, toys, jackets, and equipment that were out of style, and he was looking for some way to dispose of them.

The doctor's mother asked her son if Project Partner could use any of these materials. You know Chuck's answer. The next week a semi-trailer load of Disney tee shirts was on its way to Middletown, Ohio. Oh yes, Chuck saw this gift as a great thing. It would give Project Partner the opportunity to put Mickey Mouse tee shirts on children in all the places we were ministering. Chuck and I could envision scores of children in Nicaragua sporting those Mickey, Minnie, Goofy, Pluto, Donald Duck, and other tee shirts. They would love them even if they didn't know anything about the Disney characters.

Not long after, another call came in, this one asking if Chuck would like another semi-trailer load. Of course, his answer was yes. We sent shirts to children in Guatemala, Costa Rica, Peru, India, China, Romania, Russia, and other places as well. Doing so was exciting, and it was a joy to be able to provide that kind of blessing to so many children all over the world.

But there was more. The semitrailers kept rolling in until Chuck had to find another warehouse just for them. There were tons of other Disney items as well that were great but wouldn't work for the children we were serving, so he had to decide what to do with them. Well, he decided he would sell them and use the money for the ministry, with Disney's permission. It wouldn't be profitable to retail them, as that was a whole different operation and very time consuming, so he chose to wholesale them to outlets and flea markets.

Obviously Chuck needed help on this adventure, so he hired our son John to be the distributor. John met this challenge like his dad would and was soon moving the merchandise out all over Ohio, Indiana, and Kentucky. Those Disney products were a winner in adding funds to help Project Partner's medical ministry and children's ministry. Disney was most gracious and ended up sending a total of forty-two semitrailer loads of their select and desirable merchandise to Project Partner. As a thank you, we provided Disney with many pictures of the children who received the products. Chuck wanted the people at Disney to see the faces of the children and know that their gifts were actually helping people all around the world.

His Last Year

Chuck certainly didn't know that 1991–92 would be the last of his life here on earth. He was ready to do whatever, anywhere the Lord called. The medical ministry was in full swing. He had been totally healed of his heart condition and seemed healthy and ready to do anything.

That June he took a medical team to Peru to help Rev. Lener Cauper, our partner and the national pastor there. We had met Lener in 1985 at our first pastor's training conference in Lima and had committed to helping him with his ministry. Lener's base was in the high Andes in the remote city of Arequipa. The people really needed the medical help, as they were so distant from big cities and hospitals. So there Chuck went with his medical team, working with Lener to help the people with their illnesses and diseases and to share the compassion of Jesus Christ. At the end of this two-week trip, he came home bone tired, complaining of a pain in his stomach but rejoicing again in what he and the team were able to accomplish for the people and the kingdom of God.

Norway to Russia

For some time Chuck had expressed his desire to go to Norway to see the Viking ships. I needed to go to Russia to meet up with our new partner, Andrey Bondarenko. Putting these two places together and adding Sweden and Finland, we planned for a great time together.

We headed out of JFK airport in New York for Norway in September. A leader in Gospel Films, Asborn Hager, met us at the Oslo airport and volunteered to show us around his beautiful country, driving us through those majestic mountains and explaining the history of their unique fjords. He also made sure that Chuck saw as many Viking memorials as possible. A highlight was that he introduced us to several Christian groups, and we learned of their plans to reach all across Norway with the gospel.

From there we took a train on to Sweden, and again we had made arrangements to meet a Christian leader. He put our experience there into an understanding as to what Christians were doing in Stockholm and Sweden. Next was a cruise ship over to Helsinki, and on the dock was a lady waiting for us. Helsinki was everything we expected a European city to be, with its beautiful neo-classical buildings, bustling traffic, clean environment, and elegance. Our new friend showed us around a bit and then took us to the retreat where several pastors were meeting. Tapio Aaltonen was our contact. After the retreat, we had dinner with him and his family in Helsinki. Chuck and I thoroughly enjoyed being immersed in cultures this way. How fantastic to meet with our Christian brothers and sisters in these other countries.

From there we took the train into Leningrad, renamed St. Petersburg in 1991. That experience was "interesting," as we didn't speak the language. It was also frightening when soldiers came through the train and took our passports. We didn't understand Russian, and there we were without our passports. We didn't want to think about "what if?" or be filled with fear of the unknown, so we prayed for the Lord's protection.

As we waited for what would happen next, we made our way to the dining car and were shown to a table with two other people. It was typical in Russia for people to be seated with people they didn't know. Chuck could hardly believe it when the waiter gave us our bill for the dinner and it was only $1.09 for both of us. Russia was too new to being a part of the world economy to realize the difference in the value of money. Just before we arrived at our destination, the soldiers returned and gave us our passports.

In Leningrad, Andrey Bondarenko was waiting of us with a bouquet of yellow roses for me. He was very excited that we were there to see him and the work of Christians. Leningrad was quite a city then, and it is still reeling from its new freedom. In its earlier history it was a very special city with a winter palace and numerous summer palaces plus other palaces for the tsars and their families as well as a major fort to protect it from the Swedish army. It was built by Emperor Peter the Great and had been the cultural capital of Russia. It has become a beautiful show place of Russian architecture and design. Chuck was intrigued with the history, since he knew a lot about the siege of Leningrad by Hitler during World War II. That terrible siege left 641,000 dead from the cold and starvation.

Beyond the palaces and museums we could see numerous highrise buildings with "communal" apartments, each housing multitudes of families. These structures, some twenty stories high, showed major depression. They hadn't been built to last, and they were in very bad shape. It was to one of those numerous distressed buildings that Andrey took us to meet Victor and his wife, Olga. Inside we headed for the elevator, only to discover it was not working and obviously hadn't worked for some time. So our morning exercise was climbing up to the twelfth floor to meet Victor.

Walking down that dark hall to the door, Chuck was thinking about the total control Stalin once had over Russia and Hitler once had over Germany. Millions and millions of people with no freedom, no choices, just blind obedience to the government. Where they lived was dictated to them. What they ate was limited by what the government made available. Where they worked was ordered by the state. Darkness, gloom, and total control at the whim of a dictator. At this point in their history, they were free and struggling to overcome the past. To us their task seemed like digging out of a hole with only a spoon, not a shovel, but free at last to dig.

Victor was delighted to see us American Christians. He eagerly prepared some tea and bread for our lunch. Yes, it was just that—tea and bread. Nothing else, as it was their usual lunch and all they had. He shared with us his heart's desire to get the Bible into the schools in Russia. It could be done. The schools were welcoming Bibles, but the problem was getting them. As we sat in that small, dismal room, twelve stories up in that distressed building, Victor shared his heart and his dreams for promoting the message of Christ. He had survived, and he was a disciple of Jesus Christ in Russia.

Andrey then took us to the airport for a flight to Latvia. The three countries of Estonia, Latvia, and Lithuania on the west side of Russia had regained their freedom and were developing their own governments. Andrey had served Billy Graham as an interpreter in Graham's historic crusade in Moscow in 1988, and his burden was for evangelism. It was there in Riga, Latvia, that Andrey was leading churches and pastors in expanding the exposure of the people to the gospel. It was 1991, and this part of the world had just opened up to the outside world. Chuck spoke in many of the churches, and the people were eager to hear him and to know more about the Christians in other countries.

Andrey also took us to the prison there in Latvia and introduced us to the warden. Amazed that we Americans were there, he offered to show us around and to have us speak to the inmates. Yes, was Chuck's response, and why not? The warden showed us the barracks, the cells, and death row, and then he had most of the prisoners file into a large room. They were dressed in gray prison garb, heads shaved, and sat on small, wooden stools. When the warden discovered that I was the president of Project Partner, he turned and asked me to speak to them. It was a blessed opportunity to tell them who Jesus Christ is and how he could help them. It was also a great comfort to have Andrey as interpreter, since we knew he wanted to get the message across too. At the end, we were to be escorted out ahead of the prisoners but chose instead to shake hands with them one by one as they returned to their cells.

The warden then turned to Chuck and said, "I so completely believed in communism, and now it is gone. Now I want to know about this Jesus Christ. How do I find out about him and Christianity?" Chuck loved that question and gave him some answers before telling him that Andrey would be the one to share with him what Christianity is all about. Before leaving, Andrey made an appointment to come back and talk further with the warden.

That trip had been just what Chuck wanted, as it fulfilled his dream for seeing a new area of the world and sharing the gospel there.

Family Time

After returning home, Chuck had another plan. He wanted to spend time with his family. He wanted and needed some vacation time. We had been given a week at a resort in the Bahamas, so he offered his sons the opportunity of going with us there in November 1991. Paul and John were able to take him up on the plan, giving us a tremendous vacation time together. Chuck loved that. In December I needed to make some contacts in Florida, so again Chuck worked it out that he and I would take a vacation interspersed with a few appointments for me. It was just what a vacation in Florida should be.

Christmas was always special for us, and that year we were with Paul and Dawn and John and Nancy in Cicero, Indiana. Our two newest grandchildren, Michael and Morgan, loved to sit on Chuck's knee, and he loved to play with them.

Bad News Again

January 1992 arrived, and Chuck talked again about the pain in his stomach. It had been there off and on since June, but it was getting worse. Of course, he had gone to the doctor and they had run the tests, checked him over, but couldn't find any problem. He was convinced he needed to check it out further. He scheduled a test on Tuesday, January 7, 1992. The results were grim. His doctor said it appeared to be stomach cancer. They would run another test the next day to be sure.

I was scheduled to leave the next morning to take a team of ten to India. Chuck insisted that I go, as it was my responsibility. I knew that I would not be able to find someone else to lead the group on such short notice; and visas, tickets, and arrangements could not be changed. The circumstances were difficult, impossible. Bringing our pastor into the situation, we decided I would take the team on to India and he, Claude Robold, would be there for Chuck. I would get the team to India, turn the group over to Samuel Stephens, buy a return ticket for the next day, and only be gone three days.

The test results again showed stomach cancer.

Chuck was told there was no known remedy. Chemotherapy would give him only a few more months. Surgery, too, would give him only a few more months. There was no cure or permanent remission available. The doctors said he could have three to six months, but that was the best they could offer.

Understanding that his time on earth was suddenly very limited, Chuck took advantage of those three days I was gone. He made his list of what he wanted to do before he died. He was ready to meet the Lord, so his list consisted of what he wanted to do to care for his family. He wanted to make a last visit to each of his sons and their families, write a letter to each of his grandkids, do some repairs on the house, and make arrangements to take care of me.

Of course, he asked for prayer, and many came and prayed with him. He also had visitors who came from all across the U.S. as well as Nicaragua, Mexico, Costa Rica, Haiti, India, and Russia. But he only had eighty-seven days from diagnosis to the end. Those days were spent in communion with his Lord and concern for his family. He listened repeatedly to Dan McCraw's tapes of worship and praise. He quoted Paul from 2 Timothy 4:7: "I have fought the good fight, I have finished the race, I have kept the faith." It was his time to go and be with the Lord and be beyond the pain and suffering.

Having Served God's Purposes

Chuck went to be with his heavenly Father on April 1, 1992. His funeral was a time of worship and praise. Pastor Claude Robold officiated with numerous leaders from across the States as well as from around the world adding their remembrances. His internment was in the Springboro, Ohio, cemetery. His tombstone quotes Acts 13:36: "For when David had served God's purpose in his own generation, he fell asleep."

Yes, Chuck served God's purpose in his own generation. He is with the Lord, but his legacy lives on. He taught us to accept a challenge and respond with "why not?" He showed us the life of a man of integrity and purpose, a servant of the Lord God Almighty who chose to do his will, his way, and made impact on the lives of hundreds of thousands around the world. He served God in his time. He came, he lived, he was a man of God in his generation, and he passed the baton on to those following after him under the leadership of our Savior and Lord.

The story goes on. God is not finished with Chuck Thomas or his influence or his family. The Lord moves us forward in new ways, new venues, and with new ideas. With God, there is always more.

Chapter Nineteen
TRIBUTES FROM MINISTRY PARTNERS

Here are the stories of six men of God who had a special relationship with Chuck Thomas. Their ministries go on and on, blessed by his encouragement and service.

Rev. Samuel Stephens
President, India Gospel League
Salem, India

"Will you both allow me to be your father?" Whenever I think of Reverend Charles Thomas, those are the words that come very vividly to my mind. I can almost hear those words as if they were spoken just a few moments ago in Chuck's distinct, compassionate, and soft voice. The person who spoke those words is no longer with us. But those kind yet powerful and encouraging words and the spirit in which they were voiced continue to be a source of moral support and strength to us even to this day.

It was the spring of 1989. My wife, Prati, and I were returning to India after our first visit together to the United States. Chuck had come to see us off at the Cincinnati airport. We were sitting in the restaurant near the departure gate, eating the last few morsels of one of my wife's favorite foods—pizza. Of course, it was Chuck's treat.

Both of us had lost our fathers within a 12-month period between April of 1988 and February of the following year. We were still grieving. That visit with Chuck and Donna Thomas was a life-changing experience for both of us. It was the start of a new journey. The beginning of a new chapter in our lives. The opening of a new door and a new pathway.

As Chuck spoke those words, we realized he wasn't just reading our thoughts and responding in sympathy. We knew that he was able to feel our pain and loss. Being a very practical person, he wanted to reach out in the most practical way. As the days went by and we had the opportunity to get to interact with him more and know him better, that is how he came across all the time. He could never turn away from needs without doing whatever he could to meet them. That, I believe, was the hallmark of his life and his ministry. He was compassionate, considerate, and caring.

Chuck Thomas was one of the most kindhearted and gentle person I have ever known. I distinctly remember when I first met him. Chuck and Donna had just flown in from Florida after their youngest son John's wedding. They had traveled separately, and Donna had arrived home earlier. I was having supper with Donna in their home.

I remember the sound of the truck's tires on the gravel in their driveway as he arrived home. After initial introductions, he began talking about the turbulence during the flight and the difficult landing. All of a sudden he stopped and said, "Now tell me about yourself." That is the only time I can recall Chuck talking about himself unless specifically asked. He always focused on others, showing genuine interest in what others had to say and always looking for practical ways to help and to express his concern. I always felt immensely respected whenever I was with him.

Chuck was unique in the way he understood the role of nationals in ministry. During the 1980s there was a lot of talk in the West about the importance of national leaders in missions. But in my observation, the true potential lying with nationals had not been recognized. Overseas missions were still operating in the paradigms of the past. Chuck and Donna Thomas were ahead of their time. I believe they were among the first to usher in a new era of missions partnership working on an equal standing with national leaders. He fully understood the heart of nationals and was deeply committed to empowering them to carry out the vision God had given them for their respective countries.

Chuck was a great enabler. It was amazing for me, coming from an Eastern culture, to watch how he stood beside Donna, encouraging her and enabling her to lead the ministry of Project Partner. That in itself was a great learning experience for me. Encouraging others to succeed was his life's contribution to all who knew him. For me, every minute spent with him was a source of great encouragement and inspiration.

We were deep in conversation one day when he stopped me and said, "Samuel, remember, no matter where you are in the world, if you need help, I am only a phone call away." It is difficult to describe fully how I felt when I heard those words.

As a young man learning to lead a ministry and fearful of the unknown, what he said to me that day was like a shot in the arm. From that day on, along with the presence of the Lord, I had the confidence of a relationship that I could trust and lean on in times of need. It wasn't just the things he said or did, but the example he set as a man of God and the manner in which he was committed to serve the Lord and help people.

My desire was to have Chuck visit India to see the growth of the ministry during those years. He too promised me that he would come. But that dream of mine never became a reality. We had prayed and planned a possible visit in February of 1992. But his health had already deteriorated by then. I had the privilege of visiting him on several occasions during his illness. There was sacredness about him as he patiently endured the pain and discomfort.

My acquaintance and friendship with this great man of God unfortunately was very brief. It was less than five years. But in that short period of time, I was able to learn much from him. He mentored me. He had allowed me the privilege and freedom to approach him any time for counsel help and guidance.

Certainly Chuck Thomas was one of those incredible people who leave an indelible mark upon people's lives for good. He has left a deep impression on my life. I owe a lot to Rev. Charles Thomas for what I am and the way the Lord is using me in his vineyard today.

Dr. Enrique Cepeda
Executive Director, Thomas School of International Studies
Mid-America Christian University, Oklahoma City, Oklahoma

In 1964 when I was a student at Gulf Coast Bible College (GBC), Dr. Max Gaulke, the president, told me that a pastor in Wichita, Kansas, was looking for an interpreter to go to Mexico with a group of people to make a missionary trip. He recommended me. This is the way I was presented to Rev. Charles F. and Donna Thomas, who were pastoring the Pawnee Avenue Church of God. Dr. Gaulke himself took me all the way to Anderson, Indiana, to meet them at the annual convention of the

Church of God. Little did I know that this relationship was going to become a lifelong relationship.

Let me share some of the events and highlights in my relation with the Thomases.

- I remember very well that every summer before we made a missionary trip to Mexico, I stayed with Chuck and Donna Thomas and discovered that they have the gift of hospitality. Even when I was out of school in the summers, I knew that their home was my home. Every time I was in town, either in Kansas or Ohio, they would not let me stay in any other home but in theirs. This I treasure very much in my heart. They became my American parents.

- When I married Lydia, my Mexico City girlfriend of nine years whom I met when I was studying there for the ministry, Chuck took the time to prepare me. He gave me lessons that not only helped me in my marriage, but helped Lydia and me in teaching hundreds of couples that we have prepared for marriage in the last twenty-five years. Ninety-nine percent of the couples that we have prepared are still together in their marriage, for which we thank the Lord and Chuck, who took the time to teach me these valuable lessons.

- The same year that I was married (1969), I was also ordained in the ministry. When I invited Chuck and Donna to be in my ordination ceremony, Chuck said, "I do not have time, but I will make time to be at your ordination in Ensenada, Mexico." Chuck and Donna flew their Cessna airplane there, and he prayed the ordination prayer for me. I remember very well that prayer, especially when he asked the Lord for me to be faithful. God has answered that prayer, helping me to be faithful to my calling, to the ministry, and to my wife, Lydia. His prayer is still ringing in my heart today!

- Chuck was also a man of vision. He told me before Project Partner was founded, "Enrique, I am going to establish a missionary agency, and I want you to be part of it." I was then with CNEC (Christian National Evangelism Commission), which is now Partners International. I remember how in 1981 I became part of Project Partner to help in the ministry of supporting nationals in their own country. I was one of them, because all my life I had lived in Mexico.

- One of the things that I like the most is to share with pastors. Project Partner gave me the opportunity to do this in Guatemala, Honduras, Nicaragua, Colombia, Peru, Argentina, and Mexico. Several times I was very privileged to interpret for Chuck. Teaching and preaching with boldness is another wonderful gift the Lord gave him.

- His Classroom Without Walls was another adventure that we lived together, both in Mexico City and Guatemala City. Students came for a month or so to study the culture and the language and to live in that city. Warner Southern College issued college credit. I traveled all the way to Guatemala with Lydia and our first two daughters, Liz and Myrna, to be part of this experience. There I saw another quality in Chuck's character. He was very creative and was able to approach a need, a task, or an idea from a new perspective. An experience never to be forgotten!

- When I graduated from Fuller Theological Seminary (1976) in California with my doctoral degree, it was a special gift from the Lord to see Chuck and Donna at my graduation. My parents from Mexico were not able to come because it was a long and expensive trip for them, but Chuck and Donna were there. This was very significant for me and Lydia. This is another quality in Chuck's character, his availability, where he put aside his schedule and priorities to serve others.

- Another experience that has helped me in my life was the National Leaders Congress in 1989 that Project Partner did for us. It left us with principles that will help us as long as we live. Many times I rode with Chuck in his pickup truck, and many of the lessons that I learned from him were in those short trips. It was in one of those rides that he told me about his vision for Project Partner and his dream about medical evangelism. Project Partner and Caring Partners International continue even now, so many years after he has gone to be with the Lord.

- Already I said that Chuck was a man of vision, creative, and available. I also said that he was bold, that quality where he was confident of what he said, taught, and preached. I was able to trust him completely.
- Compassion was another wonderful quality in Chuck's character because he was willing to invest whatever was necessary to heal the hurts of others. I will never forget when an earthquake hit Nicaragua, then Guatemala, and later Mexico City. He not only went to help those who had lost everything, but he influenced churches and other groups to help too. I remember when a train full of goods, water, food, and clothes was sent to Mexico City. Chuck made arrangements with the Mexican authorities for the pastors to handle all the distribution. Another example of this was Sea Angel, the medical boat in the Caribbean serving people in Guatemala, Honduras, Costa Rica, and Nicaragua.
- I was blessed by Chuck's generosity in how he carefully managed his personal resources so that he could give to those in need. He gave of his own money to bless others even beyond the family of God. If the local church that he pastored did not have the budget to do it, he would freely give or find a way so that a project could become a reality, like the bus and the airplane.
- I noticed also that Chuck did not hold any grudge with those who did not understand what he was doing; I saw in him a spirit of forgiveness. When he established Project Partner to do what the local churches were not doing, some people misinterpreted his intentions. This did not stop Chuck doing God's will to bless thousands of people around the world. When Donna wrote the book *Climb Another Mountain* and gave the reason he founded Project Partner and results of that ministry over the years, some of those people who had misinterpreted his intentions came to her to say that they were sorry for what they had thought about Project Partner and the Thomas', that they could see they had been wrong.
- Chuck was also a man of wisdom in the way he responded to life situations from a perspective that transcends cur-

rent circumstances. I was very much blessed by his wisdom and advice that he gave me.

I just want to give thanks to God for giving me the privilege to know the Thomas'. This man left tremendous footprints in my life. Chuck was an example in such a way that has challenged me to serve my God with all my heart, all my soul, and all my strength, and to make a commitment to obey the Great Commission. I aim to please God and pray that I may influence others as Chuck has been an influence on me.

Rev. Ali Velasquez
Macedonia Vision Ministries
Nicaragua, Arkansas, Senegal, West Africa

Memoirs about the work of the Rev. Chuck Thomas, his missionary passion and service in times of crisis and need in my country, Nicaragua, during the period between 1973 after the earthquake in Managua up until his death in the 1992. Written by the Rev. Ali Velásquez, disciple and partner in missions with Project Partner and now not only serving the Hispanic Churches of Arkansas, where he now resides with his wife Dana and five of their seven children, but also in Nicaragua and in Senegal, West Africa.

Rev. Chuck Thomas was a brother, pastor, friend, licensed pilot, leader, but more than anything, a true servant of Christ with missionary passion and unrelenting in his travels, where he always sought how to help those in need.

I met the Rev. Chuck Thomas and his wife, Donna, in my beloved Nicaragua after an earthquake destroyed our capital, Managua, in a matter of seconds. There were thousands of dead and hundreds without homes on Christmas Eve of 1972. Chuck contacted Rev. Misael López and his wife, Amina, then forming a servant team to assist our National Evangelical Missionary Association in a reconstruction program to rebuild destroyed churches and the homes of pastors and to provide resources for children to study and receive biblical classes. Because of his great service, I remember his name forever.

For a while, I only knew about his faithful support to the needy in Nicaragua via my mother, since I was absent due to my continuing education studies in Spain. Upon my return in 1978, our country was still struggling through the reconstruction. Chuck and Donna Thomas practically felt as if Nicaragua was their own home, although they resided in Wichita, Kansas, where he pastored a Church of God congregation. At that time he was President of Project Partner and flying his own airplane to bring valuable donations to churches and hospitals. Chuck Thomas never saw impossible projects. His faith was his strength, and in this way he reached outside of his beloved North America. His goal was always to reach the farthest to start churches, help the pastors, and serve the community.

My country, Nicaragua, suffered an abrupt change in 1979 when a group of young sympathizers and students of Cuban and Soviet socialism overtook power in an armed revolution, which ended with the dictatorship of a family who, for more than forty years, had directed the political and economic life of a country with a high index of illiteracy. After the earthquake and the revolution, Nicaragua stood as one of the poorest countries in the world. Tidal waves and continual droughts led the weakened country into an intense search for international aid. Chuck Thomas again, without fear of a system completely different from the democracy in the United States, at his own risk, and utilizing his own plane with his wife as his co-pilot, returned to our land to help without expecting anything in return. Chuck and Donna utilized rivers and oceans as well as a hospital-ship to reach the poorest in order to bring medicine and hope. These projects were always done in partnership and in the name of Christ.

God gave Chuck Thomas the wisdom and vision to prepare those who would continue following his example of partnership ministry around the world. Project Partner was present in faraway lands such as China, India, and Peru, just to mention some. The support was essentially the same, to help with the needs and always respecting the local church leadership. This was something that Chuck Thomas always did: respect the indigenous leadership, which was the perfect formula to form a real team for Christ in each country where the Thomas couple was serving.

During that time, a tragedy hit my home that would change my life forever. For the first time, an international meeting was scheduled during the last week of October in 1989 for all the national leaders who were serving their countries in partnership with Project Partner. I lost my wife due to a tragic aviation accident when she was traveling to attend that meeting of the national leaders in Middletown, Ohio. When he heard the news, Chuck Thomas, like a friend and brother, accompanied me all the way to Miami so I could immediately return to the site of the accident in Tegucigalpa, Honduras.

God tested our vocations as servants of the kingdom, since we both had to learn not to faint and continue with the mandate. For Chuck, it was a mortal cancer, and for me, the loss of my wife. Even so, Project Partner continued being present in my country as well as the rest of the world. Finally, God called Chuck into his presence, leaving a deep pain in his beloved wife, family, and those of us who knew him closely. Up to today and for more than a decade, we remember his passion, tenacity, and example of service in faraway places, even further away than our Hispanic America.

God uses humble, courageous, and simple men to carry the truth of the gospel of Jesus Christ. The life of Chuck Thomas has been an example for thousands of people because his goal was always to disciple men and women in faraway countries with the love of Christ. I firmly believe that we can witness the work of the Holy Spirit in the character of that servant and friend who never believed in impossible projects, for God was always with him.

The Word of God shows us the effectiveness of faith and the work of his children. Chuck Thomas is certainly one of the best examples for Latin America, China, and India in that everything is possible if you believe in the person of Jesus.

Rev. Claude L. Robold
Pastor, New Covenant Church
Middletown, Ohio

Charles Thomas, parishioner, coworker, fellow servant of Jesus Christ, mentor, valued friend. I knew him as Chuck, and all these roles of his life touched mine.

My acquaintance with Chuck began when I moved to Middletown in 1980. Chuck was leading the ministry of Project Partner. I was the pastor of a local congregation. Chuck and Donna became members of our congregation, and we began a lifelong friendship.

It was a joy to discover that Chuck was a pastor's friend and encourager. His 25-plus years serving as a pastor became a great resource of wisdom to many others and to me. Our relationship intensified when we found ourselves on a church planting team together. We had earlier worked together to assist Rev. Hardy Steinke in planting a church in Mississauga, Canada. Then we found ourselves in this role. I was the church planting pastor, and Chuck was the chairman of the Elder Board.

Our visions ran parallel. Chuck's passion for many years had been to touch the world for Christ. He succeeded in doing so. My vision called for building a congregation that would touch the world for Christ. The success of this endeavor has been possible because of those early days of Chuck's foundational wisdom.

Chuck had a unique quality that was very captivating. I have been able to identify it more clearly in recent years. He knew the value of ministering to the relational needs of others. This allowed him to be effective in ministry around the world.

We all have relational needs; it is how God created us. They are: Acceptance, Approval, Appreciation, Attention, Comfort, Encouragement, Respect, Security and Support. Chuck worked diligently at ministering to these needs in the lives of others. I personally witnessed and experienced Chuck living out Hebrews 10:24, "Let us stir one another on to love and good deeds encouraging one another all the more."

The years we served together in ministry were filled with great joy. There were also times of great pain and difficulties. I learned much from Chuck as I observed him in the difficult hours of life. There came the time when he was stricken with a heart ailment that kept him from engaging in the vigorous life he so loved. His steadfastness in those days was a great example. We all rejoiced when the Lord dramatically healed him and he was able to return to active life and ministry.

The memory of the day he appeared in my office to share with me that he had just been diagnosed with terminal abdominal cancer will never be erased from my mind. He stated he had a short time and he had a plan for the days ahead. He would give himself untiringly to preparing and securing his family for his absence in the years to come. This was Chuck at his best, putting the needs of others before his own, "thinking of others more highly than himself." During the closing days of his life, our relationship was punctuated with intense and intimate conversations at his bedside that have left a lasting impression on my life.

We are told in Scripture that we have the opportunity to live life to the fullest. Chuck certainly did just that. His life was full of positive and healthy relationships. I cherish that I was privileged to be one of those blessed with a meaningful relationship with Chuck. Chuck Thomas set an example to passionately love Jesus and sacrificially serve others. He did this for my family and me, and I am forever grateful.

Lam Yam Man
Macau, China

A tribute to Chuck Thomas, the best and the most unforgettable partner of mine.

Project Partner has been building Christian medical teams to help the people in poor mountain areas of China since the 1988. China was not very much open as now in the beginning of that decade. It was not easy for an American to bring a medical team to the poor mountain areas and villages and towns, but by the grace of God, it actually happened, and a lot of people in need have been able to receive medical care from them. Chuck and Donna Thomas have been so faithful and brave in God. Their ministry has formed medical teams and taken them into Mainland (Guangdong and Guangxi) China every year. Besides, through this channel, medical equipment and technology has an opportunity to be transferred to these places. The local government has been extremely impressed.

Whenever a medical team came, it was very helpful and popular. A lot of cities were sending out invitations constantly to the team. They wished that the Christian medical team would be able to come and help them. When the team visited a city or a village, they provided the people with absolutely free medical care. When the patients knew that there was an American doctor who would be able to help them, they came to the hospital from everywhere around. A lot of people were lining up in front of the hospital. As usual there were too many patients but only few doctors. Appointments had to be scheduled from early in the morning to midnight. I was so touched and thank God for the doctors and their love to our people. The local TV station always came and reported the news of the medical team. It was a great impact of love to the local people and the officials.

I remember that one day Chuck said he would like us to pray for a 10-year-old boy. It was because his testicle shifted to another position. It was influencing his daily life and would someday influence his marriage. Therefore, it was determined that doctors should recover the testicle and move it to the correct position. However, this operation was not only difficult but also extremely dangerous. Thanks to God! He listened and answered our prayer. The operation was very successful, and the boy was healed. He is now twenty-six years old and a minister. I asked him about the medical team. He told me, "I remember Chuck, and I will never forget him and his team." Praise God! Chuck was such a person who loved God deep down in his heart. I surely believe that the God will not forget him and people will not forget him either.

I cherish my good friends and my good partners, Chuck and his wife, Donna. I respect them and I love them. They have totally offered themselves to God and set up an example for us. Finally, let me say on behalf of countless poor people in China, "Chuck and Donna, I thank you very much!"

As it is written, "Known, yet regarded as unknown; dying, and yet we live on" (2 Corinthians 6:9).

Rev. Lener Cauper
Church planter
Arequipa, Peru

I believe that Chuck understood what the Scriptures say in Luke 4:38-39. When Jesus entered Chuck's house, in other words, his heart, he immediately understood that he needed to serve like the apostle Peter's mother-in-law. When I met Chuck for the first time, I was impressed by the spirit of love and service that he had. Later, when I interacted with him, I was sure of what I had felt when I was around him. We had the same God, the same Savior, the same faith, and the same call to serve in the kingdom of God.

Chuck's coming to Peru was a great blessing. He wasn't sent as a doctor, he was just a servant. But he had authority; not man's authority, but heaven's. Chuck arrived in Peru with a team of excellent doctors, nurses, and aides. He only had one objective—to serve. He also came to help with my ministry in Arequipa, which is in southern Peru. This team came to serve more than 230 people with general medical help, emergency care, neonatal medicine, ophthalmology, minor surgeries, and other services. The patients were also blessed with receiving medicine in every appointment. Chuck was friendly with the patients, always attentive to help get the medicine they needed. The authorities of the city really thanked us for this noble gesture. He was a great friend to all, especially my family and my work team.

After two days, we traveled to Cocachacra to serve in little village on the coast. This village recognized the medical mission team for their work. A little girl had been bitten by a donkey. After the doctor stitched her up, the people of the village said, "Good job!" The medical team gave the villagers a succulent lunch and helped 180 people. The pastor of the church was very grateful. It was really wonderful to serve there.

Later we traveled to another city called Puno to help a really poor village. Once again Chuck, humble and happy, carried boxes of the doctor's medical equipment. He gave out little gifts to the children and adults, always smiling. He was the godfather of weddings in this little village, as in Peruvian weddings the bride and groom ask special family members and friends to be "godparents" of different parts of the wedding. The people only spoke Quechua, the language of the Incas. Chuck didn't understand, but his spirit just knew how to serve. He was a great example in my life and ministry. Chuck loved ice cream. He tried every kind of food. Nothing was difficult for him; he was always ready to serve. In this little town they helped 198 patients in just one day. The town leaders there were also really grateful for our help. The leader of the village recognized the medical group as sons "ilustres de Puno."

Chuck wanted to see the ruins of Machu Picchu, a historical area of Cuzco. I have wonderful memories with Chuck. We spent many tired but happy moments together. The people were blessed by this ministry. I believe that the medical team ministry should continue because it's part of evangelistic ministry. Chuck preached with his serving heart and his humility. God bless his wife, sons, and spiritual children. God bless you, Donna, for your husband. If we are faithful until death, we will be with him again. This is the Lord's promise.

Chapter Twenty
THE PATH GOES ON

Because of the vision of Chuck Thomas, a new day began across the U.S. in relationship to missionaries and national leaders and to Christians becoming personally involved in enhancing the growth of the kingdom of God in countries around the world. Today there are hundreds of thousands who go on short-term mission trips. There are now so many ways and numerous methods to get the message of Jesus Christ to the vast multitudes.

Chuck was a pioneer; however, the job is not complete. There is much more to be done. New ideas are needed. New ways of sharing the gospel. New methods for enabling Christians to partner in getting the Word of God to those who have never heard. There are still so many unreached people. If Chuck were here today, he would be asking, "Are you the one to do part of it? Is your church a missional church? The Lord has special plans for you. There are different but great ideas out there waiting for someone to tackle them. You are God's man or woman for 'such a time as this.' Seek his will, his direction, and see what he has ahead, especially for you. Seek a missional lifestyle. Why not?"

Project Partner Moves On

Yes, Project Partner moves on. What began in 1968 is going forward under new leadership. Today Rev. Gary Kendall is the president and visionary. His daughter, Kristen Levitt, is the director. Located back in Olathe, Kansas, near Kansas City, Project Partner continues to partner with local churches and leaders in the United States to spread the Good News across China. Together they demonstrate the love of Christ by meeting vital needs for drinking water, medical care, and education of rural people. They also serve the national Chinese leaders and churches across many provinces of China by providing training, teaching materials, and numerous resources.

Individuals and churches in the U.S. join them in this outstanding mission to help spread Christ's love and share the Good News. There are teams going to China and room for you to join one and do your part in making a difference for the Lord in this vast country. You can find them at www.projectpartner.org. Check it out and see what the Lord would have you do.

Caring Partners International

Would you like to join a medical team and make a difference overseas? Caring Partners is certainly doing that. What Chuck envisioned and began has grown and is serving in more countries. An unusual and blessed outreach is in Cuba. Who would have thought Christian medical teams could get in there? The new leaders of Caring Partners are Roy Cline, president and CEO, and Dr. Robert Lerer, board chair. They have opened that door wide. They have had over twenty-five medical trips to Cuba, plus the added blessing is that they are always able to give hundreds of Bibles and tracts to the eager Cuban people. Those people are searching for the truth and want to have his Word in their hands and in their hearts. Caring Partners is answering that call.

Cuba isn't the only country either. Caring Partners is serving India, Ukraine, Kenya, Thailand, Guatemala, Ecuador, and Nicaragua. New projects are being investigated in Bolivia and Brazil.

In 2008, the ministry was able to purchase a new facility and relocate its international headquarters to Franklin, Ohio. This strategic advance was so needed. Now donations from hospitals, physicians, and corporations of medical equipment, supplies, and pharmaceuticals have a great place to be processed on their way to help people in other countries. Join them at www.caringpartners.org.

Thomas School of International Studies

This school is another amazing outgrowth of the life of Chuck Thomas. That young Mexican man, Enrique Cepeda, whom Chuck brought into his heart in 1964, is now the director of this school at Mid-America Christian University in Oklahoma City, Oklahoma. Enrique earned his PhD from Fuller Seminary in California, he has a major role in Christian Business Men's Connection, and he ministers on the university level across the Western Hemisphere, training leaders for the kingdom. What a gift Enrique is in building the kingdom as he teaches students online in Venezuela, Colombia, Peru, Ecuador, Mexico, and Puerto Rico as well as here in the United States. Visit the school at www.macu.edu/tsis.

India Gospel League

What a terrific impact the India Gospel League (IGL) is having in India and Sri Lanka. From very humble beginnings in 1948, this ministry has been a faithful witness to the gospel for over fifty years. In 1992, a church-planting movement was launched; by the end of 2009, over 60,000 churches had been planted. India Gospel League currently operates eighteen orphanages, ten schools, a hospital, numerous clinics, a community college, and a school of nursing. Rev. Samuel Stephens is the president and visionary leader of IGL. He is assisted by a North American director, Dr. David Rice, and a team of over 900 dedicated workers.

Located in Salem, India, in the state of Tamil Nadu, this ministry has now spread to eighteen states with over 7,000 church planters and pastors. Through their faithful witness, thousands are coming to Christ daily. The IGL Children's Gospel Clubs (CGC) is a ministry for children launched every spring and followed by forty-two weeks of Bible study. The CGC is reaching over 500,000 children plus many of their parents, bringing them into a relationship with Jesus Christ. James 2:5 (NIV) aptly describes the ministry of the India Gospel League: "Has not God chosen those who are poor in the eyes of the world to be rich in faith and inherit the kingdom he promised those who love him?" Learn more at www.iglworld.org.

Macedonia Vision International

From the time of his youth and after the destruction by an earthquake of Managua, Nicaragua, in 1972, Reverend Ali Velasquez began to work in association with Project Partner. They worked together bringing assistance to the AMEN churches, hospitals, and pastors; and they rebuilt churches. In 1996, Ali decided to leave his world as a businessman and dedicate his life to serving the Lord full time. He came to the United States with his family and began to study at the Hispanic Baptist Theological Seminary in San Antonio, Texas. Upon completing his studies, he moved to South Carolina, where he served as director of Hispanic church planting among Baptist churches for almost seven years.

Feeling the call to international service, Ali established Macedonia Vision International in 2003 with my assistance to serve Mexico, Central America, and the Caribbean in training pastors and church planting. Since 2008, he has been working in association with numerous Baptist churches from other states to adopt the tribes of the Wolof, Fulani, and Sereer in Senegal, West Africa. They participate in community service projects and evangelism for these ethnic groups, which have not been reached by the gospel of Christ.

Presently Ali serves as pastor of Betel Hispanic Baptist Church in North Little Rock, Arkansas. He and his wife, Dana, and their seven children and two grandchildren live in the United States, where they serve the nations in presenting Christ as the Savior of the world as Jesus mandated. Ali can be reached at Ali@alivelasquez.com.

Heart to Honduras

It was 1989 at a meeting under a grove of trees in a remote village. Charlie Smith met with Miguel, his wife, Nilsa, and a dozen pastors from different denominations to see if they were interested in forming an association for mutual support and ongoing pastoral ministry. Following the model he had seen in Nicaragua with his mentoring pastor Misael Lopez's partnership with Chuck Thomas and Project Partner, Miguel began hosting teams of North Americans to work with this new network of churches.

Charlie Smith's leadership impacted Miguel, and upon his death, the ministry leadership fell on Miguel's shoulders. The ministry includes a medical clinic serving a dozen villages in addition to medical, dental, and surgical visiting teams from the States. The School of Discipleship has trained nearly 200 young men and women from Central America, Colombia, and Haiti for pastoral and evangelical work. There are agricultural and home improvement programs as well as youth programs and ministries. Miguel serves approximately thirty churches across Central America. The seeds planted through Chuck's work with Misael Lopez in Nicaragua, which resulted in Miguel Pinell's journey to the States, are translating into souls and lives saved today and, through the School of Discipleship, well into the future.

Gordon Garrett, the president of Heart to Honduras, resides in Xenia, Ohio, and may be reached at ggarrett@hth.org. The ministry Web site is www.hth.org.

Ministry to Russians

Andrey Bondarenko and his productive ministry Light in the East goes and grows. Not only is he working in Russia and the Ukraine but also from coast to coast across the United States with new immigrants from Eastern Europe. Andrey and his wife, Natalia, were planting churches, holding tent meetings, and leading Christians in Latvia until 1999, when that government would not let him continue, as he was actually from Russia. Moving to California, they are now serving thousands with his preaching and teaching in churches and various venues.

Andrey also has a tent ministry in Russia and the Ukraine, and every year they hold large-scale missionary events where thousands of people gather to hear the Good News of salvation. Through Light in the East, they also provide Christian literature and materials, motivating Christians for involvement in serving the Lord in almost all the former Soviet Union countries. Andrey and Natalia reside in Lake Forest, California. Andrey can be reached at lftl@cox.net.

Lener Cauper, Pastor/Leader in Peru

The Andes in South America are remote and difficult, but Lener Cauper and his wife, Herma, natives of Peru, know this is where they are to serve the Lord. Located in the southern part of Peru at Arequipa, they are planting churches, developing leaders, training pastors, and dedicated to taking the gospel to every area. They do not have a base now in the United States, making it more difficult, but that isn't stopping them from producing for the kingdom. Lener is the recognized leader of numerous churches across Peru and is also training his sons to follow in his footsteps. Chuck Thomas's last medical team trip was with Lener in Arequipa in 1991. Lener can be reached at lcauper@hotmail.com.

Missio Link International

Romania has been through much turmoil with the previous communist government, and the country is still recovering from that past. Chuck made a trip to Romania in 1990 where he saw the need and the potential. Soon the Lord raised up Eugen Groza to be the Lord's disciple in reaching the people groups in that country. Romania has a history of children needing care, training, and homes. The pastors also need training and encouragement. Eugen's ministry is serving these needs. I was greatly encouraged to see the scope of this ministry in a recent trip to Timisoara.

In 2008, Eugen stepped down as the senior pastor at Bethany Baptist Church to dedicate his full-time work to the various ministries at Missio Link International (MLI). Eugen is taking this ministry beyond the borders of the churches and to the multitude of needs in that country.

Eugen lives in Timisoara with his wife, Mihala. They have two daughters, Adelina and Serina. Adelina is married to Jonathon, and they are expecting their second child in April 2010. Serena is a first-year medical school student in Timisoara.

MLI is a ministry that focuses on five areas: church partnership; leadership development; children at risk (e.g., battered young girls); Alpinis camp and retreat center; and Agape programs (e.g., "meals on wheels" for elderly). More information on these ministry areas is available on the web site: www.missiolink.org.

Jesus, the Hope of Romania

Peter Dugulescu had the vision, and immediately after the revolution of 1989, founded this ministry. With all the confusion and chaos at that time, he knew that Jesus was the only hope for Romania. Chuck heard about Peter and was quite impressed as he visited his ministry in 1990. Peter was opening new doors and creating great opportunities for the Word of the Lord to be desired and followed. My visit there a few years later enabled us to endorse his ministry even more.

Peter's unexpected death in January 2008 left Ligia Dugulescu, his daughter, to rise to the task. Ligia is moving his ministry forward across Romania, ministering to the handicapped children, the orphans of whom there are many in Romania, the widows, and the poor. Her heart is in tune with the Lord in proclaiming the gospel and planting new churches in the Timisoara area and beyond. The ministry is searching for teams to come and help them in any area of the ministry, knowing Jesus is the only hope of Romania. You may reach this ministry by visiting www.isussperantaromaniei.ro (the Romania words for Jesus, Hope of Romania).

Guillermo Villanueva, Evangelist, Mexico and Latin America

Guillermo is a full-time evangelist and became a part of Project Partner in 1988. Along with his wife, Betty, he reaches thousands of people for Christ with the churches and for the churches and through evangelistic crusades in the Spanish-speaking world. He and his wife have held more than 1,000 crusades and have seen over 90,000 people coming to know the Lord. They have preached in almost all Latin America, Cuba, Canada, the United States, and Spain.

Together they also produce two evangelistic radio programs, which are broadcasted in nine countries, including United States. They counsel people personally, write evangelistic literature, and teach, in congresses and seminars, everything related to evangelism. Guillermo gives Project Partner, led by Chuck and Donna Thomas, appreciation for being a vital part of the success of their ministry. Visit him at www.guillermovillanueva.org.

Charles (Chuck) Mark Thomas

Chuck, like his father, continues to question the status quo. Believing that every work and endeavor is an opportunity to be a witness to God's grace and redemptive power, Chuck began his career seeking to be "salt" in the music and advertising business. He learned to apply Scripture to advertising and created the VALCORT® creative branding process, a unique brand-building strategy that creates trust among customers and employees by living rightly and humbly as taught in Ecclesiastes, Proverbs, and the Sermon on the Mount (Matt 5–7).

Living in Chicago with wife, Sue, and raising their four children there, he has used VALCORT to influence top industry leaders across hundreds of businesses and millions of their customers. He has generated well over 30 billion audience impressions representing such brands as AT&T, McDonald's, Toyota, State Farm Insurance, M&M Mars, the Indianapolis Colts, and the San Francisco Giants; nonprofits and ministries such as Awana, KidsPeace, Opportunity International; and local organizations including Circle Urban Ministries, Riverwoods Christian Centers, and Elgin Youth Symphony Orchestra.

Presently three of Chuck's children are married. Heather and her husband, Nathan, are ministers of music in Peoria, Illinois, where they live with their two sons. Erin and her husband, Steve, are youth leaders in Baraboo, Wisconsin. Bryson and his wife, Lexie, are in the U.S. Air Force stationed in Wichita Falls, Texas. Daughter Allie will attend Southern Illinois University.

Paul Stanley Thomas

Paul Thomas studied mathematics and computers in college and had a very successful career in information technology for many years, becoming a partner in a national consulting firm. Paul made a major decision to retire at age fifty in order to spend more time with his wife, Dawn, and their two sons before the sons go off to college. Paul's love for music inspired him to form a small jazz ensemble to play at weddings and other upscale occasions, which he greatly enjoys.

Both Paul and Dawn are very active in their church with Paul being an elder and also a part of the morning worship musicians and Dawn a part of the welcoming team as well as caring for people with special needs. Dawn has homeschooled their two sons, Michael and Johnny, as well as planned many travel vacations to broaden their sons' knowledge of the United States. They reside in Carmel, Indiana. Michael is studying electrical engineering at Northern Arizona University. Johnny is soon entering high school.

John David Thomas

John Thomas loves to help people. His desire always was to be a doctor. Although there were obstacles in his path, he followed his dream with the encouragement of his wife, Nancy. He received his medical degree after studying in Indiana Wesleyan University, American University of the Caribbean in St. Maarten, and Providence Hospital in Michigan. Presently he is the hospitalist in Longview, Texas, where he is thoroughly enjoying serving the sick and caring for the afflicted.

On the top of his accomplishments John lists his marriage to Nancy Holland and their three children. Nancy earned her PhD in Psychology at Ball State University in Indiana. Morgan Dawn, their oldest daughter, is studying international business at LeTourneau University in Texas. Martin is busy writing band music and playing in several bands during his high school years. Nicole, also in high school, is moving along with her interest in horses. John says his life purpose is to serve the Lord, to care for his family, and to be of service to those that are sick. He and his family reside in Longview, Texas.

Afterword

Does one's influence cease at death? Hardly. Good or bad, it lives on. In the case of Chuck Thomas, his influence, encouragement, and endorsement have impacted his wife, Donna, in every aspect of her life, both in their years together and in her years of ministry since his passing. She has said, "I am in the Lord's service, and I cannot retire or quit. It is in my heart and my blood, and I seek to serve him every day of my life."

Ordination

Donna had never considered ordination, but since she was training pastors in numerous places during the years of Chuck's illness, it was brought to her attention that she should consider it. Chuck urged her to do so, and so she contacted the ordination committee for their opinion. They readily agreed. On October 25, 1988, she was ordained as a minister of the gospel of Jesus Christ by the Church of God of Anderson, Indiana. At the service were pastors from Presbyterian, Methodist, Evangelical Free, Baptist, and Nazarene churches, people she had worked with over the years in ministry. Dr. Herbert Kane, retired missionary to China as well as professor at Trinity Theological Seminary, was there. Chuck and all the board members and staff of Project Partner as well as five national pastors were there to pray with her. It was an affirmation that she was to continue serving the ministry of Project Partner and national pastors, helping them take the gospel to the remote areas of the world.

National Pastors Training

One of the outstanding programs Donna continued to develop after Chuck's passing was the training of national pastors. She took that ministry on to numerous countries, and it was always eagerly received and appreciated. I was on her second trip to India and have been back twenty times. If we could count the number of pastors trained over the years in all the countries where Donna established this program, it would be an astounding number. This program has been especially productive because it trains pastors who train their leaders who train their people. The effects go on and on and on. It is impossible to know how many millions of people over the years have been reached with the gospel as a result of it. Yes, training native pastors and leaders is the way to go. It produces for the Lord in ways we can never imagine.

Partnering with National Leaders

Another program that Donna continued to develop after Chuck's passing is partnerships with national leaders. When Donna became president of Project Partner, the ministry was still going strong with short-term mission trips, or work camps, as they were called then. As more and more churches and leaders began picking up the concept and running with it on their own, the Lord turned Donna's focus to partnering with productive national leaders. She turned the ministry of Project Partner to these national leaders, starting with Enrique Cepeda in Mexico, then Pastor Lam and his outstanding ministry across China, and then Samuel Stephens and all his teams in India.

In 1987, at a national pastors training conference in Cochen, India, Donna introduced Rev. Jim Lyon, now pastor of Madison Park Church of God in Anderson, Indiana, to this ministry. In 1994, she worked with Samuel Stephens to form the U.S. non-profit corporation, India Gospel League, North America. Jim Lyon is currently chair of its board. Through his role as a speaker for Christians Broadcasting Hope, Jim has endorsed this ministry repeatedly, thereby helping its growth. I now serve as vice chair of this ministry.

Donna went on to establish partnerships with Ali Velasquez in Nicaragua, Lener Cauper in Peru, Joe Surin in Haiti, Guillermo Villanueva in Latin America, Peter Dugulescu in Romania, Andrey Bondarenko in Russia and Latvia, and Eugen Groza in Romania, all great men of God.

An added blessing to these relationships is that Donna is now the "American Grandmother" to many of the children of these national leaders. This very special relationship started with Becky and Daniel Stephens in India and Timothy and Caleb Lam in China, and it now includes children of all the national leaders mentioned here as well as some in Saudi Arabia, Senegal, and Guinea.

Cuba 2004

If you want to get people's attention, talk about Cuba. What happened to Project Partner's team there in 1974, how the Lord intervened, was nothing short of a miracle. However, you can't mention Cuba without telling the whole story—then and now. What a joy and privilege to retell that first story, since it gives another opportunity to tell how the Lord has worked things out for his glory since then.

Donna returned to Cuba in 2004 with Caring Partners International, the medical ministry that had previously been a part of Project Partner. It was the ministry's eighth year of twice-a-year or more mission trips to Cuba. Donna joined the team in Miami and then flew to Cancun and on to Havana. No problem with immigration because the team was registered as a medical evangelical team with equipment, medicines, and doctors to teach in the hospitals. Nancy, a high level functionary of the Cuban Ministry of Health, and Victor, Tomas, and Ramon, Baptist Church representatives, were there to meet them.

The team's purpose, in addition to sharing the Good News, was for the physicians on the team to lecture and to give testimony to Cuban doctors and health care workers in six different hospitals in western Cuba. Arriving at each hospital, the team members were welcomed by the hospitals directors. The medicine and equipment was presented, the agenda discussed, and then the directors were asked if the team could distribute Bibles. In every case they were more than welcomed, were able to hand out Bibles in every room, and every hospital director wanted a Bible as well.

The most amazing aspect to Donna on the whole trip was the receptivity of the gospel. Everyone wanted a Bible. When services were held, the churches were packed, and often there were three or four sermons given by the team. On the average, twenty to fifty people come forward to accept Christ at each place.

Yes, Castro's regime is still in power as it was when Project Partner's plane was forced down there 1974. Thirty years later, however, Christians are delivering the Word and Bibles to the Cuban people with absolutely no fear or problem. Chuck Thomas would be so proud and happy to know about it. Chuck thoroughly enjoyed telling about his Cuba experience and how the Lord worked it all out for good. Donna thoroughly enjoys telling how the Lord is working in Cuba today. Only the Lord could have used both of these encounters in such an outstanding way.

Writing and Consulting

Donna retired from Project Partner in 1999 as the Lord was moving her into a new career—a career of writing and speaking and consulting. In 2000, she established Christian Vision Ministries. By then there were so many stories of Chuck and her ministry that people started asking Donna to write a book about them. *Climb Another Mountain,* her first commercially published book, came into being and was published by Warner Press in 2001. It was followed in 2004 by *Becoming a World Changing Family,* which was published by Baker Books and later picked up by YWAM. Then *Faces in the Crowd,* published by New Hope Publishers in 2008, made the news in *Outreach* magazine, *Christianity Today,* and numerous other publications. Before all of these books, however, in 1994 she self-published her journal for short-term missions, *Through the Eyes of Christ,* for the purpose of helping those on a mission trip discover what the Lord is trying to teach them. It continues to be revised and used across the country.

Many leaders of ministries and especially leaders developing new ministries have sought out Donna for advice and ongoing consulting. To date she has served eight ministries in obtaining their 501c3 status with the IRS, including Caring Partners International; India Gospel League, NA; Doulos Ministries; Mission Resources International; Grace on Wings; Macedonia Vision International; Repair the Breach Ministries; and Heavenly C Ministries.

Speaking

But there is more. Donna is now blessed to speak in many different venues, from churches to conferences, universities, assemblies, and conventions. The Lord also has opened the door for her to speak on Harvest TV and REJOICE TV and on Decision radio, CBH Viewpoint radio, Moody radio, and others.

Donna has been a chapel speaker at Indiana Wesleyan University, Mid-America Christian University, Anderson University School of Theology, Warner University, Warner Pacific University, and Southern Nazarene University. She has spoken at the Indiana Homeschool Association, National Missionary Convention of the Christian Church, and other churches and conferences around the States.

Surprises

Donna would tell you that it is obviously the work of the Lord that this shy girl who married Chuck Thomas has been featured in several books and magazines. She likes to tell people that her story appears just three pages beyond Mother Teresa's (because it is placed alphabetically) in Shirley Brosius' book, *Sisterhood of Faith*. There are also stories of her life in *Add Life to Your Years* by Ted Engstrom, *Divine Assignments* by Lana Heightley, and *Just Beyond the Passage* by David Liverett. She has also been featured in *Outreach Magazine, Christianity Today, Carmel Currents, Indianapolis Woman,* and *Focus on the Family* magazine.

The Legacy Continues

This book and the story of Chuck Thomas' life and ministry end here, but the vision and legacy of this man of vision will continue for many generations. Donna and I both now serve on the board of Mid-America University, the publisher of this book. It is our prayer that the stories in these pages will inspire many more generations of missional leaders like Chuck Thomas.

Rev. Claude Robold
January 2010